Parliament and the Media

CHATHAM HOUSE PAPERS

The Royal Institute of International Affairs, at Chatham House in London, has provided an impartial forum for discussion and debate on current international issues for over 75 years. Its resident research fellows, specialized information resources, and range of publications, conferences, and meetings span the fields of international politics, economics, and security. The Institute is independent of government.

Chatham House Papers are short monographs on current policy problems which have been commissioned by the RIIA. In preparing the papers, authors are advised by a study group of experts convened by the RIIA, and publication of a paper indicates that the Institute regards it as an authoritative contribution to the public debate. The Institute does not, however, hold opinions of its own; the views expressed in this publication are the responsibility of the author.

CHATHAM HOUSE PAPERS

Parliament and the Media

A Study of Britain, Germany and France

Ralph Negrine

THE ROYAL INSTITUTE
OF INTERNATIONAL
AFFAIRS

Pinter
A Cassell imprint
Wellington House, 125 Strand, London WC2R 0BB
370 Lexington Avenue, New York, NY 10017-6550

First published in 1998

British Library Cataloguing-in-Publication Data
A CIP catalogue record for this book is available from the British Library.

Library of Congress Cataloging-in-Publication Data
A CIP catalogue record for this book is available from the Library of Congress.

ISBN 1-85567-556-0 (paperback)
    1-85567-555-2 (hardback)

Typeset by Koinonia Limited
Printed and bound in Great Britain by
Biddles Limited, Guildford and King's Lynn

Contents

List of tables and figures

Tables

Figures

List of tables and figures

Acknowledgments

The research presented in this study was, for much of the time, a collaborative effort. Rachel Eyre helped with the collection and analysis of data. The German data were collected and coded by Professor Dr Heribert Scatz and Volker Greger at the Rhein-Ruhr-Institut für Sozialforschung and Politikberatung (RISP), University of Duisburg. The French data were collected and coded by Professor Jacques Gerstle and his team at the University of Paris, and by Professor Remy Rieffel and his team at the Institut Français de Presse, Université Panthéon-Assas, Paris. Further help was provided by Virginie Le Torrec.

This project would not have been possible without the generous help provided by the Headley Trust. I wish to record my gratitude for their support throughout. I would also like to acknowledge the kind help and advice given by Professor Jack Spence at the Royal Institute of International Affairs throughout the duration of the study. His patience was much appreciated. Further help and advice was given by George Joffé at the Institute. Others contributed to the project in numerous ways: my thanks to Anders Hansen for his help with the data processing, to the journalists and Members of Parliament who gave me their time, and to the many others who helped me with the administration of the project.

Ralph Negrine

About the author

Dr Ralph Negrine is Senior Lecturer at the Centre for Mass Communication Research, University of Leicester. He has published widely on politics and the media, including *Politics and the Mass Media in Britain* (2nd edition, 1994, Routledge) and *The Communication of Politics* (1996, Sage Publishers). Other publications include books on cable television and satellite broadcasting.

Chapter 1

Introduction: a decline in parliamentary coverage?

In 1993, Jack Straw, the Labour Member of Parliament, published a short research report which outlined the ways in which the press coverage of the British parliament had been substantially reduced in very recent years. More specifically, it identified the ways in which parliamentary debates were now hardly covered, if at all, in major national broadsheet newspapers. Announcing his findings, Jack Straw observed that until about 1988, parliamentary debates had received between 400 and 800 lines of daily coverage in *The Times*. By 1992, coverage had declined to fewer than 100 lines (Wintour, 1993). But the report also sought to contrast the range of activities reported in *Hansard* with the range of activities reported in the press, and here too it found the press coverage wanting. By identifying these changes, the report thus drew attention to the sheer absence of items which reported debates, announcements, intentions to introduce bills and the like: items, in other words, which offered information on a variety of matters going on in parliament and particularly in the Chamber of the House itself. In this way, the report merely emphasized just how much parliamentary activity was now *no longer* being given any coverage whatsoever.

Although the Straw report had many methodological weaknesses, it received a fair amount of publicity and it helped to bring to the public's attention the ways in which the coverage of parliament had changed, and not necessarily for the better, over a fairly short period.

That report, however, was not the only event in the early 1990s which helped to bring this topic to the fore. In 1991, Simon Jenkins, then editor of *The Times*, took the decision to end the practice of carrying extracts

1

from speeches, among other things, on that newspaper's dedicated parliamentary page. When subsequently asked in 1995 by the Nolan Committee on Standards in Public Life about his decision to do away with that paper's parliamentary page in 1991, he admitted that he had decided to abolish it because he could not find anyone 'apart from Members of Parliament' who read it. He went on to make two further statements which, with hindsight, mark the fracturing of a set of implicit assumptions about the triangular relationship between the British parliament, the press and the public. 'We are not there', he continued, 'to provide a public service for a particular profession or, for that matter, for a particular chamber. ... Newspapers are about providing people with news.' By the mid-1990s, then, no British daily newspaper had a dedicated parliamentary page or section which included verbatim extracts from speeches made by Members of Parliament in the House of Commons.

Whilst the journalistic explanation had some merit, if only as far as journalists themselves were concerned, Jenkins's decision and the evidence published in the Straw report were received differently by others. Jack Straw, for instance, saw the decline in coverage as a sign of the lessening importance of the role of parliament within society as a whole, as an indication of a declining interest in the nature of debate in the chamber and in argument *per se* and as a general comment on how a key political institution was now viewed, at least as far as the main channels of political communication were concerned.

The repercussions of the decline in coverage could also be framed within a broader agenda, an agenda which took in not only parliament but also the democratic process as a whole. As one British MP interviewed for this project put it:

> If this institution [parliament] is precious for the fabric of the future of our society then I believe newspapers should reconsider at a senior level if they are making the sort of contribution that they should be making towards the maintenance of our parliamentary democracy. (Member of Parliament, 1996)

This perspective helps to redress the balance away from journalistic explanations for changes in coverage, but it also begins to highlight the tensions which often underpin the relationship between the worlds of politics and the worlds of the mass media (see, for example, Seymour-Ure, 1979; Negrine, 1996; Blumler, 1991). Political actors need, and so seek, publicity through the media so as to reach a wider public; but the media, perhaps increasingly, make decisions about what to cover on grounds of whether those speeches, events or whatever are deemed to be 'newsworthy'. They do not simply wish 'to provide a public service for a particular profession or, for that matter, for a particular chamber', to use Simon Jenkins's phrase.

So, as more and more media attention turns to the in-fighting and the confrontational part of political life, to the examples of manipulation and control of communication by both politicians and the media (see, for example, Jones, 1996), less attention is devoted to those aspects of parliamentary and political life which cannot easily be turned into dramatic headlines. In media terms, so this argument runs, a raucous Prime Minister's Question Time (PMQT) redolent with appropriate 'sound-bites' is likely to be worth more than a sober, though none the less informative, committee sitting in the House of Commons.

David Taras, writing about the coverage of the Canadian parliament and politics, provides the most extreme of comments to describe this sort of shift and its impact on practices; with the 'old' medium of television, he writes:

Journalists rather than politicians became the stars of the show. This could be seen in how the daily activities of parliament and legislatures were portrayed to the public. Journalists sought out the sharpest conflicts, the most sensational charges and the most outrageous gaffes and politicians were more than able to supply these in quantity. (1996: 7)

From this perspective, then, the concern is that only parts of the richness of political institutional life will be represented in the public media, and that the decisions as to which parts are represented will be made by the media with media considerations in mind. Furthermore, that what is represented in the media is less and less the 'actuality' of parliaments – the speeches and debates, or the day-to-day work of members of parliament – and more and more the mediation of parliament and politics by the media. The media 'filtering process', predicated as it is on some notion of what is/is not newsworthy, then creates an image of parliamentary and political life which is, at best, a restricted view of a complex and much larger process of deliberation and law-making.

If the media have wound down their coverage of parliamentary institutions and of politics more generally, it follows that the public will find out less and less about what goes on in parliamentary institutions unless, of course, the events are deemed to be newsworthy. The day-to-day activity of legislators will, by contrast, be defined as uninteresting and not worthy of column centimetres. By giving publicity to issues raised in parliaments, the media explicitly acknowledge the importance of those issues; but by ignoring them, the issues, and perhaps the institutions themselves, disappear. One British MP tells the story of how his visitors from Hong Kong took comfort when they heard the parliamentary debates on the handover of their territory to China in 1997, but that they were dismayed to find nothing of the debate mentioned in the following day's press.

One effect of such a pattern of coverage on members of parliamentary institutions was offered by a German parliamentary correspondent interviewed in the course of this research in 1997:

> There is sometimes the impression, particularly among the members [of the Bundestag] that there is a lack of sufficient awareness. They say that they are wearing themselves out to no effect and that journalists write about the government and about certain appearances by particular people and that insufficient respect is paid to their work. They would like to read something like a reflection of the parliamentary process in the newspaper.

This is not to minimize the difficulties the media face when attempting to cover parliamentary institutions that are complex and events that are part of much larger processes. However, difficulties should not be reasons for giving up practices, particularly in those instances where others believe that key democratic principles may be at stake. As the British MP interviewed remarked, the media need to consider what contribution *they themselves* are making towards the maintenance of parliamentary democracy when they give parliament and politics the coverage which they do. To this MP, the decline in the press coverage of the British parliament represented a changing perception of its significance within the democratic process and, by extension, a changing perception of its significance in society and for the public as a whole.

The contrasting views offered above – those of political actors as against those of journalists – simplify what is, in reality, a much more complex set of problems: problems relating to changes in media and to changes in political institutions. It also takes for granted two assumptions which need to be scrutinized more critically. The first assumption is that there has been a decline in media coverage of parliamentary institutions and that the extent of that decline can be easily determined; the second is that the decline, where this has been documented, is in itself reprehensible.

In the case of the first assumption, and as Chapter 5 will show, there has never been a time when concern has not been expressed about changes in parliamentary coverage. There never has been, in other words, an agreed adequate or acceptable level of coverage. A historical perspective on this matter is therefore essential. In the case of the second assumption, it is open to question whether, say, an extract from a speech in a parliamentary institution is superior, or preferable, to a journalistic interpretation of that same speech which also places it in a broader political context. As with the first assumption, there are important qualifications which force us to reconsider what appear, at first sight, to be uncomplicated positions.

The research reported in this volume seeks to provide answers to many of the questions relating to the changing nature of parliamentary coverage and of political coverage more generally which have been posed above, either explicitly or implicitly. But it seeks to do something else as well. The concerns discussed above have purposely focused on the British political environment, yet the changes referred to may have their parallels in other countries. The additional task, then, was to examine whether the changes reported in the British context were similar to changes taking place elsewhere, or whether they were more, or less, extreme.

All these considerations helped to frame the research design and also to formulate the key questions which guided the analysis of print and broadcast media. Three specific research questions stood out.

- Has there been a change in the nature of the coverage of parliamentary institutions and of politics more generally in the recent past and, if so, what has been the nature of that change?
- Are political actors, consequently, gaining less direct access to the columns of newspapers or to television air-time?
- What are the possible reasons for any of the changes identified?

Alongside these questions there were some others which were less easily answered through quantitative research but which still needed to be considered, if only in passing, in a study such as this. These included the following.

- How 'adequately' do the media cover and/or reflect parliamentary institutions and their work?
- Are there better, and different, ways of covering political and parliamentary life?
- Are contemporary public perceptions of parliament as an institution and of politics as an activity somehow related to the nature of the coverage currently available? If, to use a specific example, all the viewing public ever gets to see of the British House of Commons Chamber is a rowdy Prime Minister's Question Time, is it able to build up a rounded picture of parliament and its work? In this respect, what needs to be considered is not simply what, or how much, *is* broadcast and its character, but also what, and how much, *is not*.
- Are there similarities between the way the media in different countries cover politics and parliamentary institutions and is there a convergence of media practices across countries?

In order to explore the major research questions, a selection of media from Britain, Germany and France was chosen for analysis. These media included the main evening television news bulletins (for example, BBC 1's *Nine O'Clock News*, ZDF's *Heute*) and some of the major broadsheet or elite newspapers (*Guardian*, *Frankfurter Allgemeine Zeitung*, *Le Monde*) from two distinct periods, that is, from 1986 and from 1996. In this way, it was possible not only to chart change across a decade and but also to examine changes across different political and media systems. Further details of the content analysis, as well as of the media selected for this study, can be found in Chapter 4.

It would be wrong, however, to suggest that the focus of attention in a study such as this should be entirely on the media. As will become clear later on, journalists often express the belief that the media are reflecting the *changing*, and the *changed*, role of parliamentary institutions in modern democratic systems; reflecting in their practices, in other words, a change and often a decline in the role of a primary political institution. As a former editor of a national broadsheet paper remarked:

> There are only a very small number of debates which actually matter. The rest is the outward and visible show, but in a newspaper you cannot do everything on its own self-evaluation.

In this remark, one finds an appreciation of the changing nature of parliamentary life (in the reference to the general *un*importance of parliamentary debates and to the 'outward and visible show') and an understanding of the changes brought upon newspapers (in respect of changing newspaper priorities). Or, as a senior broadsheet newspaper reporter explained it in 1996:

> Parliamentary reporting is a casualty and part of the context in which newspapers change. It has not been singled out. It's the sort of service where people will say: 'No, sorry. This does not justify the cost.'

Seen in this wider context, the critical issues that need to be considered here are not simply about the changing media world or the changing world of politics, but the changing interplay between the two continually evolving worlds of the media and politics. The outcome of these changes and of the interplay between the worlds of the media and of politics is, perhaps, the current state of political and parliamentary coverage.

The structure of this volume

The major research findings from the analysis of media content are set out in Chapters 5–8. Chapter 2 provides an overview of the changing nature of parliamentary coverage in the three countries chosen for this study. Chapter 3 sets out the methodology of this study, while Chapter 4 looks in greater detail at the changing nature of parliamentary and political coverage in Britain. Chapter 9 offers a conclusion and a summary of the results across the three countries examined.

Chapter 2

The changing coverage of parliamentary institutions

In the introductory chapter, a number of references were made to media practices *vis-à-vis* the coverage of parliamentary institutions and political coverage more generally both in Britain and in other countries. This chapter aims to provide a general overview of some of the relevant research on this topic as a way of identifying the broader global trends which have had an impact on the interplay between the world of the media and the world of politics. Two important points about such comparative overviews must be borne in mind. The first is that there may be significant differences between media (for example, press versus television) within countries as well as across countries, and this necessitates a broader appreciation of the media systems of particular countries. The second is that there are often significant differences between the roles and status of similarly named and similarly constituted political institutions in different countries and that, consequently, one is not always looking at identical institutions. Therefore, one should not expect the nature of the coverage of parliamentary institutions to be *a priori* the same or similar. This second point is discussed more fully below (pp. 24–28). The next two sections examine some findings in this general research area drawn from studies of the press and of television.

Changes in newspaper coverage

Although events in the 1990s alerted a wide audience to changes in the nature of political and parliamentary coverage in Britain, there was by then already a substantial body of evidence which had documented this

Table 2.1: Coverage of parliament in three regional dailies, 1900–72*

	Yorkshire Post		Manchester Guardian/ Guardian		The Scotsman	
			Coverage as % of			
	Total space	*Total editorial*	*Total space*	*Total editorial*	*Total space*	*Total editorial*
1900	–	–	7.6	11.4	6.3	9.6
1912	5.3	6.9	8.4	12.0	6.7	10.2
1924	5.5	7.6	5.8	8.0	5.9	9.8
1936	3.8	4.7	4.1	5.2	6.2	8.0
1948	1.7	2.1	8.3	12.0	6.7	10.6
1960	2.0	3.4	3.3	5.3	3.6	5.8
1972	1.6	2.9	3.0	4.3	3.9	4.8

*Sample: Ten days in each parliamentary session.

fact. In his mid-1970s study of regional newspaper content across several decades at the turn of this century, Colin Seymour-Ure concluded that a pattern of decline in parliamentary coverage could be dated back to the 1920s and 1930s and that by the 1970s, parliamentary coverage was considerably lower than it had been in the period between the two World Wars (1977: 113; see Table 2.1).

A different study, this time for the 1976 British Royal Commission on the Press, found that in the 1970s, parliamentary debates constituted 3% of the news sections of the broadsheet press, while the category of home political, social and economic news comprised 19% (McQuail, 1977: 29). Although the 3% given over to parliamentary debates may have been small, one could still argue that its sheer existence had an important symbolic and even political significance. By the 1990s, even that 3% had disappeared!

Other research into the longer-term changes taking place in the way newspapers treat political, social and economic affairs – of which parliamentary news items are usually considered to be a part – suggested that the underlying trend was for the print media to move away from such content and to place an increasing emphasis on human-interest stories (see Negrine, 1994: Chs 3–4, for a discussion of this). More recently, there have also been suggestions that newspapers have become more tabloid both in their content and in their approach to news, with a greater emphasis being placed on personalities and conflict, and greater use of photographs, larger headlines, etc. (see Engel, 1996). Such changes perhaps underpin the more specific changes which are of particular interest here. Clearly, if there has been a trend towards tabloidization, then it is the coverage of political news and parliamentary items in their many forms which was likely to suffer most or has suffered most.

Research in other countries has also thrown up a number of observations that help us to understand the sorts of processes which have affected parliamentary and political coverage generally. Two such observations are particularly noteworthy. The first is the changing nature of coverage as observed in the American context. According to Timothy Cook:

> The diminution of newsmaking on the House [of Representatives] floor revealed and reinforced new political priorities. The earlier preference for debates, recorded with little interpretation or comment, had been founded on an egalitarianism that opened up the process of the people's branch to all for scrutiny. By the end of the [nineteenth] century the correspondent had emerged as one who would make sense of the goings-on of Capitol Hill for a mass audience that was perceived to demand colour and excitement more than details of policy disputes. (1989: 22)

Subsequent changes in the balance of power within Congress, and the emergence of a more visible and active presidency, further diminished the attention which was once paid to the House of Representatives. The intrusion of the broadcast media merely reinforced this trend by concentrating on leaders and on conflict even further and at the expense of attention to debate and discussion (Cook, 1989: Chs 1–3).

The second observation relates to changing priorities in news. From his own research, Stephen Hess has suggested that one of the reasons for the move away from Congressional coverage was the cost of having correspondents based in Washington. Another was that 'the [newspaper's] home office had a vision of what *consumers* wanted that differed from the opinions of the field office [the journalists]' (1994: 146; emphasis added). The end result of all this was not only a downgrading of Congressional news in the broadcast and print media – and Hess quotes Penn Kimball's research which is critical of how little the networks cover Congress – but also 'a re-evaluation of what is news on the part of the mainstream American publications' (1994: 147). As he puts it:

... newspapers and television are now almost as likely to feature stories about business, education, health, religion, or culture as about what is happening in Congress and the other branches of government. (1994: 148)

So, not only are there strong organizational arguments for not carrying political news in the same way as before but there is also a tendency for a broadened agenda to feature on the front pages. While part of that agenda may be political in a non-institutional sense, for example about the environment or about education, it was also likely to be more interpretive than in the past. As the German parliamentary correspondent put it in 1997:

Today, unlike previous days when the reporting was more conventional and sympathetic and there was simply more straightforward reproduction, you have to put the material into a journalistic form. You have to adapt the material in order to convey the essential information from the flood of news.

There is, perhaps, more than a hint of the changes identified by Stephen Hess (1994) in the data collected for this study. In all three British broadsheet newspapers analysed (*Guardian, Financial Times, Daily Telegraph*), there was a reduction in the number of political items appearing on their front pages between 1986 and 1996. In 1986, 13% of all the primary political items, that is, items involving political actors in a dominant capacity, coded for the *Financial Times* appeared on its front pages but this figure had gone down to 10% a decade later. The figures for the other newspapers are more dramatic: in the case of the *Guardian*, 21% of all the primary political items coded appeared on its front pages in 1986, but only 13% of all coded items in 1996; the figures for the *Telegraph* are 25% and 18% respectively. From this sort of evidence, it would be easy to argue that the place of politics in the life of the newspaper has changed, though there is another consideration here which further complicates any such conclusion. In this ten-year period, British newspapers have themselves undergone enormous change. One such change has been the greater use of larger photographs, larger headlines and fewer stories on the front page. Consequently, there are fewer stories on front pages today than there were ten years ago, so the decline in the number of political stories on the front pages is part of a much larger process of change. Nevertheless, the point remains that the front pages are less likely to carry as many *political* items as a decade earlier.

Research from other European countries, where available, appears to point in the same direction and also to a longer-term concern about the changing roles of parliamentary institutions themselves. In a 1968 symposium on parliaments and media organized by the Inter-Parliamentary Union, much concern was expressed about the widening divisions between peoples and their parliaments. One of the major themes developed in the subsequent report was the need for parliaments to pay closer attention to their communication needs and to their need to communicate. At the time, one should recall, Britain was one of the few West European countries not to allow broadcasting from its parliament and much of the discussion in the symposium centred on the advantages and disadvantages of letting broadcasting into the institution. Another interesting aspect of the report was the growing awareness of a changing relationship between media and parliaments as new media came on stream. Where radio and television were developing rapidly:

> The new media already threaten to elbow out the press from its old function of factual reporting. To some observers this signifies the relegation of the printed word to either a mere record or to a supererogatory task of comment by journalists no better qualified to interpret parliament than any other reasonably educated citizen ... (Wilson, 1970: 26)

As one delegate remarked:

> I think that the evolution of the different information media ... will gradually result in a decrease in news *reports* in the press, as its role will become that of *commenting* on the news. It is obvious that radio and television broadcast news and that the only role left for the press is that of commenting on events ...
>
> I think therefore that verbatim reports of parliamentary proceedings in the press run counter to this necessary evolution, and that we should not be surprised to see less space allocated to parliamentary proceedings. In my opinion this does not constitute a lack of responsibility. It is just an indication that the press has realised that things have changed, and they no longer have to report the news. (Wilson, 1970: 34)

Was there any evidence to support this position? The evidence is sketchy and suggestive. On the one hand, it is clear that extensive reports of proceedings were already in decline in both France and (West) Germany before the introduction of broadcasting into the respective parliamentary institutions. In the case of Germany, Oberreuter has suggested that press reporting of parliamentary proceedings was carried on a daily basis in the nineteenth century, 'under a permanently established column in the press' but that '[b]eginning with the Weimar Republic, the press started to select subject matter and debate according to their importance' (1990: 527). By 1971, Hennis could write (about West Germany) that, 'we know, of course, that *the times are long past* when the great newspapers would publish full-page parliamentary reports' (1971: 77; emphasis added). In the period under investigation here (1986 and 1996), press reports of the parliamentary institution (Bundestag) were integrated into the normal domestic political coverage of the newspapers.

Another delegate suggested something not dissimilar about France. Pointing out that only the small-circulation *Le Monde* devoted 'two pages a day to verbatim reports of parliamentary proceedings', he went on to observe that it 'scarcely pays to write about such a serious subject as parliament for *the general public*. We have come far since the day when a fine French newspaper, *Le Journal des Débats*, showed by its title the importance it attached in its columns to parliamentary proceedings' (1970: 31; emphasis added). By the 1980s, even *Le Monde* had ceased to cover proceedings as it had done previously (Padioleau, 1985: 238). In a more general vein, Charon points to the *dépolitisation* of the French press (1991: 131–3).

This downgrading of parliamentary reporting in the press clearly stretches back to several decades before the 1980s, but it may have accelerated once the television cameras moved into the respective debating chambers: in the 1950s in the case of West Germany, the early 1980s in the case of France but only in 1989 in the case of the British House of Commons. After all, if the important speeches and events were being broadcast, there would be little point in the press providing a print version of something which had already been seen by millions in news programmes. It may be more than a coincidence, then, that the rapid downgrading of parliamentary news items in Britain happened so soon after the introduction of television into the House of Commons in 1989. Indeed, it could be that the late arrival of television into the House actually *prolonged* the tradition of verbatim coverage of parliamentary proceedings in the British press by comparison with practices in other countries.

A final factor which might help explain why British coverage has been so prolonged may be the nature of the British parliament itself, a parliament which generates sufficient political conflict and dissent to give the press something to write about. As Hennis pointed out in 1971 with respect to the German Bundestag:

> ... if parliamentary debates were to be conducted in a [different way], there is no doubt that the press and the public would be far more attentive than they are. If MPs complain that the German press takes little notice of the Bundestag, they should find fault not with the press but first of all with themselves. A parliament which holds as few public sessions as the Bundestag cannot claim the right to be a frequent object of newspaper reporting. (1971: 77)

Hennis's perceptive comments tackle the question not only of the content of debates but also of their form, and he does both within a consideration of the procedures of the Bundestag. In this way, he alerts us to the way in which institutions themselves impact on the work of the media. Similar points could also be made of the French media, which appear to display little interest in the proceedings of the National Assembly (of Deputies) (see Frears, 1990), although this may be due, in part, to the greater importance attached to the offices of the president and prime minister and the lesser importance attached to the parliamentary institution *per se* (see also below, pp. 24–28).

Changes in television coverage

If the press has pulled back from covering parliamentary institutions, what of the medium of television? Much of the empirical evidence concerning the broadcast coverage of parliamentary institutions has come, perhaps not surprisingly, from countries which have had a long experience of the broadcasting of parliamentary institutions. Britain, in this respect, is an exception; television has only relatively recently entered the House and so there is as yet no longitudinal study which has looked at changes over a significant period of time. The available published studies have focused mainly on the early years of coverage, roughly between 1989 and 1993, and they have all tended to agree that British television does a fairly reasonable job of reporting the British parliament (see Franklin, 1992; Blumler *et al.*, 1989; Ryle, 1991). As the points of reference are close together, there is not the comparison over time which might have turned up possible and significant changes in patterns of coverage.

Nevertheless, it could be argued that British terrestrial television does not offer a very large 'window' on parliament. The BBC's coverage in a typical week in the mid-1990s, for example, would include very few programmes which were solely devoted to 'live' transmissions or, indeed, recorded 'highlights'. One example of such a programme would be the mid-afternoon *Westminster with Nick Ross*, although even here the live inserts from the House are only a part of a more general political programme. The other (commercial) television channels offered less. In other words, the total time British terrestrial television devotes to actual live transmissions is quite limited, certainly in comparison to an actual day of parliamentary work. The advent of the Parliamentary Channel on cable television systems has clearly made a significant difference to parliament's visibility on television.

The case of German broadcasting is very different on two counts: first, with respect to the number of available studies on this topic; and, second, in terms of the amount of coverage of the Bundestag which could be found on German television. According to Oberreuter, the broadcasting of the proceedings of the German Bundestag is extensive and averages between 19 and 25% of the total time taken up by the plenary sessions themselves. A more detailed piece of research carried out by Mayntz (1993) confirms the extensiveness of that coverage. He calculated that there were over 318 hours of live transmissions of plenary sessions of the Bundestag in the period 1987–90, with just over 144 hours in the period 1953–7.

In order to assess whether or not reports of the Bundestag had any presence in television news programmes, Mayntz carried out a separate analysis of news programmes in 1989. He concluded that in an average week when the Bundestag is in session, the public broadcaster ARD devotes 1 minute and 24 seconds (out of a news programme of 14 minutes and 28 seconds, or 9.7%) to parliamentary reports. These he defined as reports about 'plenary sessions, committees and parliamentary fractions (or parties) of the Bundestag'. Of the other channels, the public broadcaster ZDF devoted 8.7% to parliamentary reports, while the commercial broadcasters RTL Plus and Sat1 devoted 5.3% and 1.9% respectively. Mayntz also suggests that contemporary coverage (that is, in 1989) was much more extensive than in earlier decades (1993: 358–63).

A comparison of the 'proportions of sittings, topics, speakers and speeches in the chamber of the Bundestag' represented in individual

Table 2.2: Proportion of sittings, topics, speakers and speeches in the chamber of the Bundestag reported in a selection of media, 1989 (%)

	Days of sittings (n = 150)	Topics (n = 150)	Speakers (n = 400)	Speeches (n = 1246)
Bundestag	100	100	100	100
Süddeutsche Zeitung (SDZ)	93	53	35	20
Frankfurter Allgemeine Zeitung (FAZ)	93	39	37	19
Bild	37	9	4	2
ARD	81	24	8	5
ZDF	93	25	10	6
RTL Plus	48	11	3	2

media in 1989 (1993: 364) provided some interesting contrasts between different types of media (see Table 2.2). The differences between media – elite (*FAZ*) and tabloid (*Bild*), public broadcasters (ARD) and commercial (RTL Plus) – are clearly evident. More importantly, and this is the conclusion which Mayntz emphasizes, the research shows that the Bundestag *has* a presence in the main media, although one could argue about whether that presence could be greater than it is. Heribert Schatz (1992) confirms the pattern identified by Mayntz and his data show a fairly steady rate of coverage of the Bundestag on the main television channels.

In both these pieces of research, however, there are indications that the relationship between the world of politics and the world of the media has not been an untroubled one. The former has been cautious about television's intrusion into its affairs and the changes that it could bring about, and the latter has at times been keen to make the institution more amenable to television. The outcome has not necessarily been in favour of the parliamentary institution even though the coverage of the Bundestag remains at a satisfactory level. As Mayntz observes:

The years of overwhelming interest, with hour-long broadcasts from the plenary sessions on both channels, were followed by years with better organization, when the companies took turns to broadcast in the morning or to present the evening summaries. *This development finally resulted in the fact that the reporting was almost exclusively*

limited to live transmissions and the evening summaries were no
longer prepared in the form of special reports but in a significantly
condensed form within the evening news magazines Tagesthemen
and Heute-journal. (1993: 359–60; emphasis added)

A more recent study by Barbara Pfetsch (1996) of changes in news
programmes in the German broadcasting system is discussed in Chapter
8, when it is reviewed in the context of the findings from the analysis of
the German broadcast media.

One final consideration links both press and broadcast coverage. The
media's selection process inevitably privileges some and not others, be
they subjects or people, and so not every member of parliament gets an
opportunity to appear in print or on the air. In the case of Germany,
Schatz reported that 'the bulk of media attention' was given to 'no more
than 10% of the House membership' (Schatz, 1992: 248) and others have
observed how it tends to favour the government over other players
(Oberreuter, 1990: 528). In the case of the United States, Stephen Hess
reports that the 'top third' of the senators 'represent 80% of the entire
Senate's media score' (Hess, 1986: 57). A study of the American
Congress also points to the concentration of coverage on a quarter or just
over of all representatives (Cook, 1989: 60). Whether this reflects simply
a 'publicity hierarchy', as Schatz suggests, rather than an acknowledg-
ment of different amounts of power exercised by different politicians, for
example front bench as against back-benchers and party in power as
against party in opposition, or personalities as against 'non-personalities',
is clearly an important question which needs to be explored.

In general, then, the limited research which is currently available does
tend to support the view that press coverage of parliamentary institutions
has changed considerably in recent years but that television's coverage
remains at a level which many deem to be satisfactory. This is not to
suggest that more could not be done but that broadcasting is perhaps less
a cause of concern at present. As regards the press, it is possible to argue
that a more restricted view of parliamentary institutions and thus of
politics more generally is now available.

The research reported here is intended to provide a more coherent
overview on the issue of the decline of parliamentary coverage by
exploring it across three European countries using a common framework
for analysis. This is discussed more fully in the next chapter.

Chapter 3

The content analysis

The evidence reported in earlier chapters tends to confirm that there has been a change in parliamentary coverage and political coverage more generally, particularly as far as the press is concerned. That evidence, however, generalizes across media sectors and so fails to distinguish different patterns of change which may be visible, say, within the press as a whole. (One exception to this is the study by Mayntz, which does take account of different types of media.) Furthermore, it rarely makes visible the very real methodological issues which make comparisons over time and across countries so difficult. Finally, it rarely questions some of the assumptions made by those who see any decline as reprehensible in itself. These three specific issues will be dealt with in this chapter, which also outlines the methodology adopted for this particular study.

The selection of media for analysis

The first of the three research questions outlined in Chapter 1 was perhaps the simplest to ask:

- Has there been a change in the nature of the coverage of parliamentary institutions in the recent past and, if so, what has been the nature of that change?

To try to answer this question, it was necessary to make comparisons across media and across time. Selecting media for analysis was easier than selecting the periods for comparison. Both the press and the broadcast media have undergone enormous changes in recent years. The press, especially the British press, has gone through a process of change: in design terms, in organizational terms, in terms of the more competitive environment. But so, too, has broadcasting with the advent of new non-terrestrial channels. Consequently, it was important to select the periods for analysis in such a way as to reflect periods of relative calm on either side of periods of significant change. Hence, the choice of 1986 and 1996 as years for comparison: the former antedated the sort of severe competition which is now commonplace in the media world, while the latter represents the more competitive era. In all three countries, the mid-1980s still largely represented a period in which the terrestrial, public broadcasters reigned supreme. By contrast, the mid-1990s are representative of severe competition, with satellite and cable services eroding the dominance of the public broadcasters. For Britain, the two years chosen also fall either side of a dramatic change in parliamentary coverage, namely, the introduction of television cameras into the House of Commons in 1989.

The media chosen for the content analysis from the two main sample years of 1986 and 1996 for the purpose of comparing their parliamentary and political output are listed below. The newspaper analysis is based on 15 issues drawn from a three-month period on a rolling week basis, while the broadcast media analysis is based on two full weeks of television news programmes, each week drawn from a different month in that particular year. (Further details can be found in Appendix 1.)

In Britain
- Newspapers: *Guardian, Daily Telegraph* and *Financial Times.*
- Television: ITN's *News at Ten*, Channel 4's *Channel Four News*, BBC1's *Nine O'Clock News*, BBC *Midlands Today*, ITV's *Central News* and *Sky News.*

In Germany
- Newspapers: *Frankfurter Allgemeine Zeitung (FAZ), Süddeutsche Zeitung (SDZ).*
- Television: Arbeitsgemeinschaft der Rundfunkanstalten Deutschlands (ARD) (*Taggeschau*), Zweites Deutsches Fernsehen (ZDF) (*Heute*).

In France
- Newspapers: *Le Figaro, Le Monde, Libération* (for 1996 only).
- Television: Antenne 2/France 2 (A2/F2), Télévision Française 1 (TF1).

One further criterion guided the sampling procedure: it was important to select periods when the parliaments were in session so as to pursue the main research question set out above. A period when the parliaments were not in session would have provided no real measure of changes in the nature and extent of parliamentary coverage. Unfortunately, as not all the parliaments are in session at the same time or for equal lengths of time (see above, p. 14), the basic sample period often included days when the German Bundestag was not in session. Incidentally, this was also a problem which Mayntz (1993; see above, pp. 15–16) had to contend with.

Four other practical problems had to be confronted. The first involved difficulties in setting up a comparative study of this sort. For example, the distinction between news and features which is common in Anglo-American media is problematic in the French context where there can be a tendency to erode the boundaries between fact and comment (Chalaby, 1996).

The second problem was that despite the randomness of the selection process, certain key incidents may have played a part in giving the results reported here their particular hue. The 1996 sample period coincided with the 'BSE-beef crisis' and, in the case of France, the newspaper sample included some material on the death of former President Mitterrand. The year 1986 also was not uneventful: the 'Westland affair' involving a dispute between ministers about the funding of a helicopter manufacturer dominated the British media, as did the Labour Party's difficulties with the radical socialist group, Militant. A separate sample for 1989 – which is not reported here – was dominated by the Hillsborough tragedy in which nearly 100 football fans had been crushed to death. Inevitably, the findings reflect these events although it is possible to argue that other periods would be affected in the same way. It may thus be impossible to avoid such a clustering of incidents: when or what is a 'typical' period? A period with no crises may be deemed to be atypical but is one with many crises any more typical?

The third problem was the difficulty of retrieving old broadcast news programmes in their original form. Where there is no national media archive, as in Britain, broadcast companies archive old news programmes as items rather than as a whole: the links between items are not usually kept. This can make it difficult to provide direct comparisons of whole news programmes over time.

The final problem was, perhaps, the most difficult one to deal with. The press and broadcast media in 1986 are different from the press and broadcast media in 1996 in many ways. A content analysis which sought to examine changing patterns of parliamentary coverage would need to take this into account since it does have important consequences for how one assesses and measures the change. We shall return to this point in Chapter 4 because it has some major implications for this research.

The criteria for selecting items for the content analysis: What is a parliamentary news item? What is a political news item?

Since the aim of the study was to explore the changing nature of parliamentary coverage in the media, it was crucial to determine what counted as a parliamentary news item. There were a number of different possibilities. A parliamentary news item could be:

- an item which was *located* in a parliamentary institution or setting, for example a debate, or
- an item which involved a parliamentary actor in a parliamentary institution or setting, for example a ministerial statement, or
- an item which involved a parliamentary actor in a non-parliamentary location, for example a minister making a speech in a public forum.

Indeed, if there had been a shift away from reporting political actors (MPs, etc.) *in* a parliamentary location and towards reporting them in different and non-parliamentary settings, it was important to find a way to identify this also. Otherwise, it would not be possible to say whether the decline in the reporting of parliamentary debates or other parliamentary activities generally had been more than compensated by, say, a greater emphasis on other forms of *political*, as opposed to parliamentary, reporting.

The definition of parliamentary and political items finally adopted was similar to the one used by Bob Franklin (1995a, 1995b) in his own study of parliamentary press coverage but it was used in a much more restricted way. In Bob Franklin's study, a parliamentary news item was:

Any report predominantly appertaining to parliament or featuring an MP in any of her/his parliamentary roles, or any report where an MP is the major focus of the story in their capacity either as a member of a political party or as a private individual.

In *this* study, items which fell into Franklin's definition were coded but, and this is a significant difference, a distinction was made between those items which appeared in the dedicated parliamentary page or section and those items involving political actors which featured on other news pages. In this way, it was possible to distinguish between the disappearance of, say, verbatim accounts of speeches on the parliamentary page and other forms of political reporting which may not have suffered the sort of reduction that Straw attributed to the former category of items.

A further distinction was made within the category of political, as opposed to parliamentary, news items. Since it was possible for political actors to feature in items in a number of different ways (for example, in a dominant capacity, or, at the other extreme, to be mentioned in passing only), a distinction was drawn between *primary* political items and *secondary* political items. In effect, if a political actor featured in a minor capacity or in an incidental way in an item about an event or issue, that item would be designated as a secondary political story.

A final category of European news items was also created. In these items, the European Union featured prominently but without any domestic British political actors being involved.

These decisions and distinctions gave rise to four categories of news items, categories which were particularly useful in the analysis of the print media:

- *Parliamentary items* – i.e. items appearing on the dedicated parliamentary page or section. These were traditionally accounts of what had transpired in the House.
- *Primarily political items* – i.e. items involving political actors in a major capacity but which appeared on the news pages (henceforth primary political items).
- *Secondary political items* – i.e. items involving political actors in a minor capacity but which appeared on the news pages (henceforth secondary political items).
- *Primarily European items* – i.e. items concerning the European Union in a significant way but which made no reference to domestic British political actors.

Items in which political actors featured only briefly and in passing as a mere mention, and in stories about something else altogether, were not coded. Items which were less than three column cm. in length, that is of about 12 cm. sq. were also not coded. Such snippets of information were considered to be mainly 'fillers' and not significant sources of information or news. Finally, newspaper supplements were not coded: although these are nowadays important parts of newspapers, they tend to be based around features rather than news and so it was felt appropriate to exclude them.

Certain other categories of items involving political actors were also not coded. These included such things as cartoons, diary pieces, sketches and the like. As these have long been a staple of newspapers, it was decided to exclude them from the research reported here and to concentrate instead on the news dimension of the media. It was this, after all, that had caused much concern; the other things – the cartoons, the sketches – were long-established parts of newspapers, were taken for granted and were perhaps not likely to change significantly over the ten-year period analysed.

In practice, however, news items, particularly in newspapers, often did not neatly fit into the little boxes created for them. Especially problematic were those news items which featured British parliamentary committee reports. In theory, these should be seen as examples of how parliamentary work should be reported – except that this is not always the case. Does reporting a parliamentary committee mean

- that there is a news item about a committee report, members of the committee, etc., or
- that there is a news item about its proceedings, and the question and answers taking place *in* a parliamentary committee room?

If the latter, then one can clearly say that this is an item about a committee and its work *in a specific parliamentary location*. But if it is the former, whatever was being reported on need not be happening in a parliamentary location. Indeed, the reporter need only have access to the report itself in order to write the news item. In this case, location is problematic. The fact that the parliamentary committee is in the news is thus predicated by its newsworthiness, not by its location in the House; in which case, it becomes necessary to be more precise about the real concerns behind the argument that parliamentary coverage has changed. Is the concern about

(a) a decline in the attention given to what goes on in parliament as an institution *and as a physical location*, and to what people do within that physical location, or
(b) a decline of coverage given to those people, predominantly MPs, who belong to that institution but who can also act 'politically' outside the Palace of Westminster?

23

Returning to the parliamentary committee example just given, it is perfectly possible for reporters to cover committees (and committee reports) from an office adjacent to a good bookshop, with the use of a telephone to contact political actors for the occasional quote. Although it is not coverage of the sort identified in (a) above, it still gives a public airing to the work of MPs, as in (b). In fact, there is a strong argument for saying that the decline of the former type of reporting may not, in itself, be critical for the public understanding of parliament and politics. Much depends on what is covered rather than simply on the location of coverage. This point becomes more relevant in the context of a brief comparison of the different parliamentary systems under consideration here, something which has a bearing on the relationship between parliaments and media. It also explains why this research looks at both parliamentary coverage specifically and political coverage more generally.

A brief account of parliaments

The three institutions examined – the British House of Commons, the German Bundestag, and the French Assemblée Nationale – each play a different role within their respective political systems. In order to grasp some of those differences, it is useful to have a brief account of some of the main features of the parliamentary systems considered in this project. Such an account, however, needs to be put into a broader historical context of a growing concern about the nature and role of representative bodies faced with increasingly powerful executives. For example, where governments dominate legislative programmes, what role should parliaments play?

Part of the answer lies in how parliaments are viewed by parliamentarians themselves, by publics and by the media. In the Westminster model of parliament, the government and its parliamentary majority are one and the same and so the chamber pits a government – the majority party – against its opposition in an adversarial format. This sort of parliament is often referred to as a 'speech' parliament in order to emphasize the importance attached to the debating/discussion function of the institution. Speech parliaments are contrasted with 'work' parliaments, where the institution is separate from the government and where much of the work of government is conducted outside the plenary sessions. Work parliaments are, consequently, physically different from speech parliaments: 'members are arranged in a crescent facing the speaker president, behind whom confronting the members are the benches for the government and civil servant ...' (Paterson and Southern, 1991: 125).

The significance of this division lies in the extent to which 'political talk and conflict' is seen as a major function of the institution itself or as a desirable function of the institution. To take one example, the Bundestag adopted a version of Westminster's Question Time not only as a way of holding governments to account but also as a way of introducing a slightly different role into its procedures (see Hennis, 1971). However, Gerhard Loewenberg has argued that:

> The tradition of great parliamentary debates as the focal point of public political attention never developed in Germany as it had in Great Britain ... More recently, the appearance of new media of communication between political leaders and their constituents – party conferences, press briefings, television addresses – detracted from the parliamentary forum. Despite these traditional and contemporary obstacles to the performance of a debating function by the Bundestag, promotion of public debate continues to be a major objective of parliamentary reform in Germany. (1970: 9)

Procedures and work routines impact on patterns of media coverage: where political talk is minimal, media coverage may be beneficial to government and therefore disadvantageous to parliament. A great deal rests, therefore, on arrangements which guide and influence parliaments, political work and politicians.

The British parliament is adversarial and confrontational with the governing party on one side of the chamber and the opposition on the other, no more so than during Prime Minister's Question Time. This is an important occasion for both parties, and for the media: when the prime minister scores points, the party in power is heartened, and when the opposition strikes blows, that party's morale rises. The role of such sessions then is not simply to get hold of information and let others participate in parliamentary life but also to make political points.

There are other occasions when debate takes place in the House and when such debate can have significant impact on the fortunes of ministers, but not all speeches are deemed significant in news terms and few are made to a packed House. It is thus instructive to observe just how quickly the chamber of the House empties immediately after the end of PMQT! A rather empty chamber is perhaps more typical of the day-to-day nature of the institution and many speeches are often made in a chamber with few MPs and now even fewer, if any, journalists in attendance. The continually changing nature of procedures in the House of Commons – the Labour government of Tony Blair has changed the procedures of PMQT and rescheduled it from a twice-weekly (Tuesday and Thursday) to a once-a-week only (Wednesday) affair – has impacted on the reporting of the institution. With the proliferation of committees, there is so much more to cover (and fewer journalists to cover it all). More importantly, what MPs associate with the House and parliamentary politics, namely individual participation in political speech and political debate, has become downgraded not only as a consequence of some of these changes, for example the new committees, but also because of the complexity of modern government and the controlling power of governments as they tighten their grip on their party members.

In France, by contrast, power is divided between the president and the prime minister, who leads the majority party in the parliament, the Assemblée Nationale. Other differences, such as, say, that ministers need not be members of the parliament (that is, elected deputies), or that committees play a significant part in the scrutiny of a government's legislative programme, are important and give the French parliament its particular role – the role, according to John Frears, of an institution that is 'inadequate as an arena for political debate and as a check on the executive ...' (1990: 32). Frears goes on to state that:

> The constitutional and procedural constraints can be summarised thus: complete executive supremacy in the legislative process, severely limited opportunities for general debates criticising the government, virtually no opportunities for scrutinising executive acts and making the executive give an account of them. (1990: 33)

There are occasions for questions but these too are limited and attempts to reform them and to introduce more 'Westminster-style' question sessions have not had a marked impact on either debates or media coverage (see Stevens, 1992: 176). In general, then, the procedures of the French Assembly do not engender political debate and hence media excitement, although John Frears suggests that what is in evidence is a more general problem:

> The inadequacy of parliament as a forum is perhaps not entirely the fault of parliament – nor even of the executive. It is occasionally asked, 'If parliament is not the forum for the nation's political debate in France, what is?'. The answer seems to be that there is not

one. It is not television or radio. .... In the Fifth Republic the
executive has been remarkably free to get on with the job of governing. (1990: 38)

Both Frears and Stevens make the point that 'governments have not
normally thought it necessary to make statements to the National
Assembly about issues of political concern' (Stevens, 1992: 186). The
general verdict seems to be that the French parliament is 'a loyal workhorse, [but] poor watchdog' (Frears, 1990: 32) and that it is 'not the
pre-eminent location for political conflict and debate' (Stevens, 1992:
190). Finally, it is worth noting that, whereas the British broadcast media
attempt to balance the government (as the majority party in power) and
the opposition but also give time to the third party, the French media need
to balance three elements: the government, the majority party and the
opposition (CSA, 1997).

In the German parliament, individual political power can derive not
from the Bundestag but from the state (*Länder*) parliaments and
individual deputies 'operate subject to the approval and supervision of
the parliamentary group' (the *Fraktion*) (Paterson and Southern, 1991:
117). It is a point which Oberreuter makes more forcefully: 'the
Bundestag is establishing itself increasingly as a parliament of
parliamentary groups in which increasingly fewer individual members
are of interest to the journalists' (1993: 519). Furthermore, a considerable
amount of work goes on in committees, thereby further altering the
nature of the plenary session. As Paterson and Southern put it:

The outstanding feature of the development of the Bundestag has
been the eclipse of the plenum by the parliamentary group and committees. The plenum registers decisions taken elsewhere. (1991: 118)

Other features of the Bundestag reinforce this: 'plenary sessions are
infrequent, numbering only about 60 a year (compared to about 170 in
France and Britain), and the deputy spends the bulk of his time in party
and committee meeting'; although 'every plenary session begins with
one hour's question time (*Fragestunde*) ... (unlike PMQT) (i) a member
needs permission of his/her party group to submit a question, (ii) the
minister need not answer the question personally, (iii) it is not a testing
ground for parliamentary work' (Paterson and Southern, 1991: 119–20).
Once again, we see a different arrangement of power and political
relationships.

The above, and very brief, exploration of differences will throw some light on the data below since it highlights somewhat different relationships between the media and parliaments, politicians and the public. There is, however, a more fundamental set of questions which may need to be addressed concerning the larger topic of how the work of parliaments ought to be made public. The following two quotes – from texts produced a quarter of a century apart – should guide any work which takes off where this monograph stops:

> It is one thing to present politics as a gladiatorial conflict ... but a noisy debate can seem much more like an undignified family squabble to those who are not taking part in it. A public increasingly conditioned by government propaganda to think of decision and decisiveness as admirable ... is not likely to find the apparent 'negative' character of debate edifying. It takes longer experience than most non-politicians possess to understand that valid decisions can only emerge from conflict itself. And even old political hands are far from unanimous that the spectacle of conflict is best put on show. ... Parliament's business is 'to talk, to debate, and by its debating to procure the action it wishes on the part of the executive – the government'. But this still leaves open the question of how far and by what means the 'talk' should be publicized. (Wilson, 1970: 27)

> The routine work of members and parties and their dealing with actual problems ... does not seem to interest the media; in any case, the media are of no help in getting such activities across the threshold of public attention. Daily political life, particularly as it results in cooperation and consensus – and that certainly is the greater part of political reality – is not being conveyed and utilised by the media. (Oberreuter, 1993: 523)

Chapter 4

British parliament, British media

Some of the difficulties which lie in the path of making comparisons across time have already been mentioned in earlier chapters. This chapter explores these difficulties at greater length and within a primarily British context. In this way, it should become possible to gain a better insight into the nature of change and, perhaps more importantly, the underlying reasons for the expressed concern about changing media coverage of parliaments and politics.

The first part of this chapter sets out some of the changes which have taken place in the British press over the period between 1986 and 1996 and explores how these impact on the findings reported here. The second part provides a historical account of changing media practices – an account which commentators often overlook. The final part sets out some of the reasons which have been put forward to account for changes in parliamentary and political coverage.

Changes in media

With respect to the press, there are two main, and very visible, changes that distinguish 1996 from 1986. The first is that the broadsheet news-paper of 1996 (and of 1998) is considerably larger than its predecessor. The second is that it is also different in terms of layout and design. Both those changes are of significance for this research.

Changes in the size of newspapers
Although the newspapers of 1996 are physically larger than the

newspapers of ten years ago, it does not follow that they carry more news and information (including political news). The actual and detailed changes in the content of newspapers across such a period have yet to be fully documented, although a crude attempt was made to explore these more detailed changes as part of this study. The results illustrate the difficulties of making generalizations or of reading too much into the simple fact of change or, in this case, of expansion.

In 1986, the *Guardian* had only one main broadsheet section which was sometimes 28, sometimes 30 and sometimes 32 pages long. The *Guardian* of 1996 contained about 26 pages and one or two separate supplements of about 40 tabloid pages. For the *Telegraph*, the 1986 figures are different: it sometimes had 26 pages, sometimes 30, sometimes 34; in 1996 it contained 34, and sometimes ran to 44 pages. In other words, there is an enormous variation in the pagination of the paper. This would also be true for the *Financial Times*, although the difference in pagination between 1986 and 1996 is not great. In 1986, it came in two or three sections with each devoted to different aspects of the financial world. The main section would run to 16 or even 20 pages, with the supplements adding another 20 or so pages of job advertisements or company news. The 1996 edition is, in many respects, similar in extent, though the presentational changes give the paper a different and more 'modern' feel.

An increase in pagination, however, does not necessarily translate into more space given to text or to political items. The detailed analysis of political news items (see Chapter 5) will emphasize the changing relationship between text, headline and photos in the newspapers across the decade of analysis. Very simply, although there are more pages, there are fewer items taking up more space. More pages, thus, do not automatically translate into more *items* or more *text*; that depends on what use is made of the available space. For example, the front page of a *Guardian* sports supplement on a Saturday might nowadays consist of one half-page photograph with some text to accompany it and little else.

A simple comparison of two issues of the *Daily Telegraph* in 1986 with two in 1996 will illustrate some of the changes described above. News items of a predominantly political, social and economic character took up approximately 3,300 cm. sq. and 2,240 cm. sq. in the 1986 issues and took up 3,000 cm. sq. and 2,600 cm. sq. in 1996. Excluding supplements, this represents 7% and 4% of total news space in 1986, and 4% and 3% of space in 1996. The *Guardian*'s political, social and economic news category ranges between 3,000 and 3,800 cm. sq., while that of the *Financial Times* ranges between 1,600 and about 2,600 cm. sq. across the two years in the analysis.

These figures have to be treated with extreme caution as they are derived from a limited analysis, but they usefully illustrate two points. First, they highlight the variations which can be found from one day to another. Second, these variations take place alongside the many other changes in newspapers that have already been identified – for example, larger photographs and headlines. That said, these figures suggest that political coverage takes place within a range or a band. If a single broadsheet page has approximately 2,000 cm. sq. of usable space (excluding margins), the 1986 newspapers carried between one and two pages of political, social and economic news.

One can grasp these points better through an examination of data from the analysis of parliamentary and political coverage in 1986 and 1996 conducted for this study. Table 4.1 sets out the average daily space taken up by all the items coded for detailed analysis in these two years. The average figures represented in this table are not substantially different from the figures quoted above, although there are some obvious differences. These figures translate into a range of one to two pages of political content in 1986 and a range of just under two to just over two pages in 1996. Thus there are some similarities across the years, although overall the averages for 1996 are larger than those for 1986. (It is difficult to translate these figures as percentages of the whole newspaper given that the supplements complicate the equation: are they significant additions to the *news* content of the newspaper or are they designed to supplement the paper with other sorts of material?)

Although the data show an increase in all three cases, it is an increase that has taken place in parallel with the redesign of newspapers and consequently with a change in the way news and features are presented. As before, it is not sheer quantity that matters but the distribution of space within the quantitative increase. None the less, and on the surface, the figures contained in Table 4.1 suggest a steady state rather than either

Table 4.1: Average daily space allotted to parliamentary and political items (cm. sq.)

	1986	1996
Financial Times	2,156	3,916
Guardian	4,552	4,625
Telegraph	3,078	3,484

a significant decline or a significant increase, apart from the *Financial Times* where the increase is substantial.

Changes in design and layout
The loss of the dedicated parliamentary news page or section and changes in the amount of political news coverage have both taken place alongside other fundamental changes in the make-up of newspapers themselves. In the *Guardian* of the 1990s, for instance, it is now not uncommon to find one large photo dominating the front page, accompanied by large headlines and a modicum of text. This happens in other broadsheet dailies as well and it reflects a different way of conceptualizing the front page and of defining its use for the newspaper. It is now often a means of enticing readers faced with an increasing choice at news-stands. One effect of this change in front-page layout has been to reduce the number of stories carried there; it follows that the number of political stories which can appear on the front page will also decline or be displaced by more leisure and entertainment fare, although it has already been suggested above that the decline has perhaps been greater than expected.

Changes in design and layout can have other effects. They can reduce the number of items carried on any page since each item carried today is likely to occupy a larger space than ten years ago: a larger space because of larger headlines, larger type and the inclusion of more, and larger, photos. Paradoxically, as the layout and design have 'opened up' the newspaper, they have done away with the smaller snippets of news and information which were in evidence even ten years ago. The point of drawing attention to these differences is to underline the ways in which changes in parliamentary coverage were taking place alongside significant changes in newspapers themselves. As newspapers were made more visually attractive and journalistically interesting, the word-laden and linguistically complex debating point or government report was perhaps bound to suffer.

The changes in the organization, design, layout and size of a newspaper need not necessarily work against the parliamentary or political item, though they do have a knock-on effect. As a former newspaper editor explained:

> newspapers are now more visually attractive but it cannot be argued from that that there can be no space for parliamentary (debates) items. It is not a question of a lack of space but of what it is that the

readers want. Is there any point feeding them something which they obviously do not want and is of little relevance not only to them but to how government itself works? That is the critical issue.

Changes in broadcasting
The critical change in the period under investigation here was without doubt the introduction of television cameras into the House of Commons in 1989. This had an enormous impact on the content of news programmes (see Chapter 6). Before television cameras were allowed into the House, news programmes used a variety of techniques to convey the words of politicians when these were spoken *in* the House. One way was to show a photograph of the politician concerned on the screen and to carry an extract – usually a sound extract – with subtitles. Another way was to have the words spoken by the newsreader or journalist. Once pictures from the House became available after 1989, these practices ceased and actual footage from the House and committee rooms was used.

In other respects, as Chapter 6 will also document, there are few, if any, significant or visible differences between the news broadcasts of 1986 and those of 1996. There are stylistic differences and possibly some changes of pace and timing but the genre of news is surprisingly recognizable as the same. This is very much unlike the situation with the press, where differences are immediately visible and obvious. By 1996, the BBC and ITN were joined by *Sky News* and other international providers of news and the point to emphasize here is that it was *Sky News* which was to provide a new format for news broadcasting.

Reassessing the underlying concern about the decline in parliamentary coverage: a historical account

The newspapers of 1996 (and newspapers since) did not suffer from a lack of space which could be given over to political or parliamentary items. In fact, people like Jack Straw who have expressed a concern about the decline in parliamentary coverage suggest that in the 1980s, when newspapers were smaller, they carried more of such news. However, as Table 4.1 shows, the actual space taken up by such items – including, say, the half-page to a page of 'Yesterday in Parliament' or its equivalent – was not very great although it probably was in percentage terms: two pages out of a 32-page newspaper is clearly a higher percentage than two pages of a 26-page main section, plus two supplements.

What may better explain the reasons for the concern is not simply the reduction of space given to parliamentary items in particular – though that is undoubtedly a concern in itself – but *the changing relationship between newspapers and parliament which the demise of the parliamentary page signified* and, as a subsidiary point, the corresponding change in the ways in which politics and individual political actors are represented. As the former editor candidly observed, parliamentary debates are of little significance and have no place in a modern, competitive newspaper seeking to retain its readership.

From a parliamentary perspective, the changes have more dramatic consequences. At one level, the loss of the dedicated politics and/or parliamentary pages has meant fewer pieces from the House of Commons/Lords and it has possibly meant fewer MPs being reported or finding a presence in the public prints. But at another, and deeper, level, it has meant that parliament does not have a place *as a matter of routine* in any newspaper and that it has to fight to get in – just like everything else. Indeed, one of the strongest themes which came out in the interviews with journalists and MPs was precisely this point: that parliament, politics and debates had to fight for space in the newspaper just like other events and people and that they could not/should not occupy pride of place and should/could not expect to occupy regular space in the modern newspaper.

With this in mind, it becomes possible to see Simon Jenkins's decision not only as a dramatic break with tradition but also, paradoxically, as the culmination of a long process of change. It is worth recalling that the political press in the nineteenth century was aimed at a very small part of the population and that only recently has the growth of its modern equivalent, the broadsheet press, attracted such considerable numbers of readers. But even in the older political newspapers the place of parliamentary news was never secure (despite myths to the contrary). Alan Lee observed that as early as the 1890s, there was a struggle within news organizations between satisfying their adopted roles as agencies of enlightenment and as commercial products serving the market-place:

> ... the provision of [politicians' speeches] was an expensive and, in terms of circulation, an unrewarding affair. They began, therefore, to rely increasingly on the services of the agencies. The agencies relied on being able to sell their reports profitably. At first they offered a choice of 'verbatim', 'full' and 'summary' reports. ... By the 1880s, the 'verbatim' was becoming rare. ... (1976: 123)

There would always be those who harked back to an earlier period. In his *Life, Journalism and Politics* J. A. Spender, editor of the *Westminster Gazette* at the turn of the century, records that it would have been unthinkable that the major politicians of the last century 'should receive less than the full honours of a verbatim report, and we were often in grave doubt whether we were doing right in reducing others to a column *in the third person*. Often we came out with five solid columns of the utterances of these eminent things ...' (1927: 35–6; emphasis added). Echoing Spender, Wickham Steed added in 1938 that 'the space now given to politics has steadily declined. ... Now parliamentary reports are condensed and treated under different headings; and in the most widely-circulated newspapers parliamentary speeches are hardly reported at all' (1938: 170).

The dilemma – to report or not to report parliamentary speeches – manifested itself even in the 1970s. The experienced political journalist John Cole recalls that when he was a candidate for the editorship of the *Guardian*, he was asked

> whether I would increase the space given to the paper's parliamentary coverage. I had to say I would not. My recollection is that at that time we gave a daily average of five broadsheet columns – about 4,000 to 5,000 words – to straight reporting of parliament. In our impecunious case, this was mostly sub-edited news agency copy. (1996)

Cole's recollections are interesting because they emphasize the 'just about right' attitude to the place of parliament in the *Guardian*, even though it was acknowledged by all that it was not widely read by its readers. It was, Cole comments, 'a service for those readers who wanted it' and it was justified in those terms. The other interesting point to note is that the *Guardian* relied on the news agencies, not its own gallery staff. One journalist interviewed for this project claimed that it was only in the mid-1980s that resources were put into a gallery role for one of the *Guardian*'s reporters. A similar alteration in news practices can be observed in the case of the *Financial Times* which, according to Kynaston, did not 'start ... daily reports of parliamentary proceedings' until the late 1960s (Kynaston, 1988: 353).

Historically, then, the place of the parliamentary report in newspapers has been problematic for many, if not for all, newspapers. The above quotes, and those earlier, emphasize the changing relationship between parliament and the press. As Wickham Steed comments tartly, the press fought for the right to report parliament but, once in, it lost interest in reporting and began to treat parliament and politicians in a different way, and in less reverential or deferential tones.

This brief historical exegesis suggests that perhaps there can never be a proper measure of how parliament ought to be reported unless, that is, one distinguishes between it and other institutions and claims very different treatment for it. If such claims cannot be upheld, then parliament needs to consider other ways of organizing its public communication either via the media or by bypassing the media altogether through, say, the use of the Internet. The press, as we have seen, decided collectively in the last century that it would mediate parliamentary content; it has now ceased to act as a 'minute taker' of debates and statements and has since consciously avoided that role. It may now be up to parliament and parliamentarians to think of ways of giving themselves a different public profile and, at the same time, making the institution more accessible.

The loss of the parliamentary page – now ably reproduced on the British parliament's web site – has been more of a loss to MPs than it has been to journalists. Many of the latter interviewed felt that reports of debates were in themselves unsatisfactory because they provided no context and no background and hence no real journalistic explanation of what was at issue in the world of politics. Furthermore, many argued, there was nowadays little point in reproducing extracts from them in print when they could be either accessed electronically or, if particularly newsworthy, seen on the main television news programmes. And so the more the broadcast media cover parliament, the less reason there is for the print media to do so. Whether these arguments by print journalists have much substance to them is open to argument since they can also be used to justify decisions already taken.

Yet television has also come in for severe criticism, though not always from parliamentarians who often see it as one medium that actually gives politics some prominence. In a letter to the *Guardian* in 1994, Sheena McDonald described the 'paradoxical state of British broadcast media'. She continued:

> A swelling tide of so-called analysis programmes provide countless platforms for publicity-hungry politicians and 'personality'-infatuated commentators to lock horns or indulge in blokeish locker room banter. In contrast, the speeches, debates and committee meetings which enable their shadow-boxing get very short shrift. ... (1994)

McDonald may, however, be out of step with the views of most producers or journalists in broadcasting if Nicholas Jones is to be believed. In his book *Soundbites and Spin Doctors* he writes of many broadcasters and MPs having an 'unspoken acknowledgement that the televised proceedings on their own were rarely sufficient to sustain full-length parliamentary programmes'. Hence, the use of interviews on College Green, directly opposite the House of Commons, and other places. And as news editors became 'bored with pictures of the chamber', less parliamentary footage was used (1996: 17). According to Jones, the increased boredom amongst broadcasters, MPs and viewers produced a sea-change in the content of parliamentary and political programmes. The move was 'away from straight reporting and the use of prerecorded material towards a greater involvement of programme presenters and many more live interviews' (1996: 18). It is curious to note at this point that French television journalists appear to have a similar boredom threshold. As one observed:

> We deal with parliament when we feel that something is happening, that a subject has to be covered. As far as the editorial staff is concerned, parliamentary news is boring but there is a lot of other news that is also boring. Viewers are not really interested in parliamentary items. I don't think this is due to the institutional dimension of such news. Items on parliament always look the same and this may be part of the explanation: the Right will be in favour of a bill, but the Left will oppose it. So it's not worth reporting. Consequently, we just report on parliament when debates occur within the Left or within the Right. (Interview, 1997)

The changes, so well documented by Jones, have clearly been to the detriment of parliament, and the place of parliament within the political system. This is not to deny that parliament itself has in any case changed in significant ways but to reiterate how television may have speeded up the process and even the direction of change. One such change, and it is one that Jones discusses, is the increased use of sound-bites: if it is sound-bites that broadcasters want, it is sound-bites that politicians will provide.

In a curious fashion, then, rather than lending support to the argument that change was inevitable and desirable, Jones's argument can be used to produce quite a different case: it is the broadcasters who are 'bored' and 'disenchanted', who seek new and exciting ways to liven up their programmes, who think up ever more ingenious link-ups and bust-ups. And as with newspapers, audience research is wheeled in to show how the public supports what could be seen as the emergence of politics as yet another part of the entertainment and leisure industry. As Sheena McDonald concluded in her letter, for the sake of voters and the democratic process, parliamentary proceedings ought to have equal time 'to that enjoyed by the pundits, spin-doctors and purveyors of flannel whose agitations presently win airtime' (1994).

The sense of journalists almost dictating the nature of news coverage for self-imposed reasons – boredom, disenchantment, a feeling that debates lack pace, etc. – can also be found in some of the views of French broadcasters interviewed for this study. A chief editor for France 2 – with many years of experience – explained how the present form of parliamentary coverage differs from that of the previous decades when 'the reporter would introduce the viewers to different politicians involved in the topic of the day through successive shots. Nowadays, we look for the issues raised by the events, for a *problématique* of the news item.' He continued:

There are fewer extracts from debates and shorter ones for two reasons: professional constraints and the end of a descriptive news structure. Today, the logic of news is to question reality. In these circumstances, we will use parliamentary extracts as a quotation to lend support to the logic of the problem developed by the journalist. Furthermore, extracts from sittings are shorter because journalists have less and less time for each subject. News items are now shorter than they were 30, 20 or even ten years ago. (Interview, 1997)

Another journalist also explained the nature of parliamentary coverage in terms of the needs of television:

I don't think parliament is really suited for TV reporting. It is an institution and its activities are not dramatic enough and they take place in too restricted a space. Television journalists need to show a variety of pictures but in parliament's case, we cannot do so and so we always show the same things.

Parliamentary news-making is just like any other kind of news-making. We look for controversial and problematic situations ... we are not systematically interested in Left/Right conflicts. The most newsworthy dissents are the conflicts within the parliamentary groups or within groups of MPs from the same party or between the government and the majority group in parliament. We report more on the political game and less on the essentials of features. (Interview, 1997)

Despite these points, this television journalist and another journalist argued that television had not turned its back on parliament. It did, they maintained, continue to show an interest in parliament and to give time to parliamentary stories, even though the emphasis of coverage and the essence of the coverage may have changed. As the third reporter pointed out, the way news about parliament and politics is now handled enables other voices to be heard. It is not simply focused on parliamentary actors and it allows for a more rounded picture. There are different nuances in all these extracts and the interviewees emphasized slightly different aspects of one problem area. All were agreed on the way television coverage tended to focus much more on conflict – though two did stress that when subjects were important the substance *and* the conflict would both be covered – and all agreed that the constraints imposed by a short news programme made it very difficult to do anything more than collect sound-bites for a 90-second item.

Why has the coverage of parliamentary institutions changed?

For the journalists interviewed, the changed nature of parliamentary coverage was part of a broader canvas of changes in journalism, parliament and politics. These accounts of change reproduced some common arguments which can be distilled into three broad explanations that were often used to account for the present form of parliamentary coverage. Though these are primarily derived from a British perspective on the problem, there are some important similarities with the other countries surveyed.

The changing nature of parliament
Arguments include the following:

- A view that the nature of parliament in the late twentieth century is radically different from that same institution in earlier times. Here reference is also often made to the existence of majoritarian governments, a strong executive controlling the agenda, powerful whips restraining dissent, an absence of 'real' debate as speeches and votes change little. So less power is exercised by parliament. As one of the

French journalists quoted above observed, much of what goes on is a 'reproduction of sets of firm attitudes'.

- A view that in 1996–7 (the last two years of the Major government) – when this research was carried out – there was a 'tired' and accident-prone government in power, with a thin legislative programme and considerable in-fighting. By implication, there is little going on but confrontation and dissent. A new government with a full legislative programme would, it was often stated by the interviewees, be covered quite differently.
- A view that politicians played a part in downgrading parliament by encouraging discussions, debates and announcements *outside* the chamber. Trailing issues outside parliament, particularly in the broadcast media and *prior* to their announcement in the chamber, forced newspapers to reassess how to cover what was then said in the chamber.
- A view that MPs themselves are downgrading the importance of parliament by their non-attendance in the chamber, so giving rise to the image and reality of an empty chamber. It follows, then, that if MPs are not paying attention to what is happening in the chamber or being said there, why should the media? This point was also made by a French journalist:

> Parliament would present a more positive image of itself if MPs were attending more regularly. Parliament deserves the way we treat it. ... If there were real parliamentary debates, then we would deal more often with parliament. This is a crucial point as it is democracy which is at stake. Parliament is no longer at the heart of French democracy. It has been replaced by an illusory one, television. But television cannot be the place of democracy ... It obeys the rules of journalism and so cannot be the place of democracy. (Interview, 1997)

Or,

> There is now perhaps a more clear-sighted view of how parliament works and the back-bencher sees himself. Why don't they turn up to debates? Because there are more important things to do. There are only a very small number of debates which actually matter. The rest is the outward and visible show, but in a newspaper you cannot do everything on its own self-evaluation. (Former editor)

However, this observation about an empty chamber can be given a different interpretation: the fact that a chamber is empty does not mean that no one is watching debates or listening in. In Britain, MPs (and correspondents) have their own offices and their own monitors on which to watch debates and news programmes on which politicians appear, so they do not always need to be physically present. Furthermore, they could be elsewhere on business. Nevertheless, the empty chamber does undoubtedly imply a chamber that is not in high regard. This was a theme which Bryan Gould, the former Labour MP, expressed much concern about:

> MPs spend most of their time in work which is no doubt useful but which does not relate to, or find a focus in, the institution which is normally thought to be at the heart of parliament .... if the Chamber is no longer working properly, we have lost an important element – indeed the central element – in parliamentary government. If the Chamber is not the place where great issues and legislative detail alike are debated and decided, then parliament simply becomes a legislative machine manipulated and controlled by government. (1984: 247)

The changing nature of newspapers
The following arguments have been put forward:

- Competition between newspapers has made them more aware of the need to serve readers and give them more of what they want to read – which was probably not parliamentary proceedings. One former editor claimed that research conducted for his broadsheet paper had long confirmed this and it was one major reason why he abandoned the regular coverage of parliament so typical in the mid-1980s. This is precisely the view Jenkins (1995) has put forward many times.
- A greater need to cover a wider set of interests and concerns among readers, for example new technologies, sport, leisure, social affairs, etc., at a time when resources were/are limited.
- Newspapers did not feel the need to reproduce speeches or extracts if these, or the best extracts from them, were already in the public domain via radio or television.
- The televising of parliament showed the wider public just how few MPs turned up to debates. Television thus showed a 'downgraded' chamber. Why should newspapers then run pages of text on parliament and its debates when so few MPs paid any attention to them?

- A view that the parliamentary timetable – for instance, debates starting late in the afternoon on most days – are not best suited to newspaper routines and deadlines. The question remains, however, whether newspapers could do more to cover what has taken place earlier on in the day. Put differently, is this an explanation of why things have changed or an excuse for not doing certain things?
- Newspapers have responded to some of the above arguments – downgrading of parliament, strong government, empty chamber, alleged insignificance of most debates – and reorganized their operations in Westminster with respect to gallery reporters and lobby correspondents: the former were the debate 'note-takers', the latter the more news-driven reporters. Having done away with the gallery team of reporters, the newspaper may have strengthened the lobby team or asked it to cover more ground in a different way. For example, the *Telegraph* had four lobby correspondents and three gallery reporters in the early 1990s; by 1996 it had five lobby correspondents. This reorganization emphasized the more 'news-driven' nature of parliamentary reporting. It also integrated the Westminster team into the whole newspaper operation much more than in the days when the gallery reporters had a degree of autonomy to report things going on in parliament and, at times, to do so independently of the lobby correspondents.

As one reporter recalled:

> When I started [in this newspaper], we had [reporters] A, B, C, and I was on the news desk. They would ring up and say 'this is the story'. You would discuss it with them but you wouldn't have any information to set against their information. But now, the desks have so much more information than they used to have that they often query the judgment of the political reporter. (Interview, 1996)

The impact of television on newspapers
This was well described by a former broadcast reporter:

> The arrival of broadcasting generated more people in Millbank. This had an effect on newspapers [which were always hostile to the BBC]. It undercut the value of news published overnight. Newspapers have reacted to the impact of the broadcasting of parliament. (Interview, 1996)

It is sometimes forgotten just how large this broadcasting operation is. With well over 200 BBC employees in Millbank – more precisely, in No. 4 Millbank, a building some 100 yards from the Palace of Westminster which houses several broadcast studios servicing a range of national, regional and local programmes – there is little that can get past the organization in terms of news. This, too, may have affected the nature of political and parliamentary reporting. Politicians visit Millbank so regularly that it often appears to have replaced the Chamber of the House itself. Moreover, whereas in the past politicians would reserve their comments for parliament and not say anything prior to their statements in the House, nowadays there is little reluctance to let the Radio 4 *Today* audience know the main lines of argument before parliament. On the same day that one of the research interviews was conducted, Nicholas Soames let the media know the main lines of his statement about Gulf War syndrome in the morning, many hours prior to his statement in the House at 3.30 pm.

With television increasing its political news output and improving its channels of political communication, the print media are forced to react to the many activities of the broadcasters. In so doing, they also questioned whether reproducing 'dated' political information was in their interest and in the interest of their readers.

Some concluding remarks

For many, the response to the death of the parliamentary page was not necessarily one of sadness. For journalists, it could be justified as a reaffirmation of their role of distilling and of *putting into context* what was taking place in parliament rather than *simply reporting* it. For one lobby correspondent, debates were the 'froth' of politics. The journalists' role, he felt, was to explain and to comment. As with Timothy Cook's correspondents, the British lobby reporters were reinterpreting their role. The ones interviewed – on the whole very young – also felt that they brought a new perspective to reporting: replacing the more traditional and deferential lobby correspondent with younger, more quizzical correspondents, looking for the *problématique*.

Broadcasters have put forward their own reasons for the changing nature of coverage and some of these derive specifically from the needs of the medium for, for instance, pictures. More generally, though, there are similar views often expressed about the changing nature of the institution, the emptiness of debate and of the chamber, the growing strength of the executive, and the like.

Taken together, all the reasons given above lend support to the changes which have taken place in the press and in broadcasting. And despite the pleas of the Bryan Goulds of this world, arguments for reversing the change or for introducing formats which give more direct access to elected political actors not only appear less strong but also quaint, almost romantic. In the newly competitive media system where grabbing and retaining the attention of listeners, readers and viewers is all-important, creating media formats which bore media customers is nothing short of suicidal.

Yet counter-arguments do have some merit. Strongest among these is the idea that the mass media are important and influential institutions within our society. Hence what they do, and the way that they do things, cannot be separated from wider processes in our society. Versions of this argument have found their way into the literature on communication over the years: from the strong version that the media portray society and its players in a particular way, and thus influence our pictures of the world outside, to weaker versions that they contribute something to the way we understand how society is made up and functions. The common thread is the idea that the media do not merely report events: the way they do so comes to have an influence on the events themselves.

Parliament, it could be argued, has suffered such a fate. Stories about 'sleaze' – whether in the form of 'cash for questions', the Scott Inquiry, or lobbyists – say something about parliament, MPs and the whole parliamentary process. Not only do they tar all MPs with the same brush, but they can undermine the legitimacy of the institution. As the media continue to hold forth, the institution of parliament could be seen to be under severe attack from the outside. In such circumstances, it would be difficult indeed to claim that the coverage has no effect or influence whatsoever on public perceptions of the parliamentary process. In parenthesis, it is worth noting that the only institutions in our modern democracy which are not under intense, daily scrutiny are the media.

Some of these concerns are more relevant to the British case than to other political systems but all highlight the ways in which the relationship between the media and the parliamentary institution has changed and impacted on procedures and routines, as well as on the public's opportunities to gain information and insight into the world of politics. Inevitably, some of these are also linked.

The loss of the parliamentary page cannot easily be excused since at a simple level it does point to the fact that newspapers are carrying less of what they used to. In a competitive era, where news is equally about leisure as about politics, about people as well as policies, this may not be surprising but it is nonetheless a loss. The process can neither be halted – assuming, that is, that one could even identify all the contributory forces that brought that change about – nor probably reversed. It is this more than anything that undermines the case of those who, like Jack Straw, look back to a golden age which in practice never existed. After all, it is some 20 years ago that Michael Foot – curiously another Labour politician – was voicing a concern that parliamentary news was 'at risk'. As Seymour-Ure wrote then, although the criticisms were understandable, 'how could it be otherwise in a modern newspaper?' He continued:

> To deplore such tendencies, it can be argued, is to misunderstand the nature of politics. ... Politics has no existence apart from the communications media prevalent in society. ... With mass politics and modern technology, forms of political communication have necessarily changed. TV is the prevalent medium and inevitably tends to impose its own manners on its subjects. This is not to 'distort' politics, for there have never been politics that were not conditioned by the dominant media of the day. What Michael Foot regrets ... is not just the passing of a type of parliamentary reporting (which in principle might be reintroduced) but the passing of a type of newspaper (which could not). (1979: 114–15)

This is only part of the problem; another aspect is that the media – in particular the press but not only the press – have 'imposed their own manners on their subject', manners rooted in its operational procedures of news values, in such a way as to diminish the possibility of debate. (See Taras's quote above, p. 3.) Though it refers to television, it does have wider application.) This, too, has significant consequences. As one British journalist explained:

> The biggest problem for journalists [is] news priorities: splits [in parties] make news. Loyal differences of opinions unless dressed up as splits are not news. So MPs are being gagged unless they want to stand out. And that is a big problem because most speeches do not take on the agenda.

So MPs are effectively gagged because of media priorities, debates become less 'challenging' and hence less worthy of coverage!

45

Many of these issues are larger than the one this study seeks to address. Nevertheless, the more restricted concern of the passing away of a type of newspaper is still worthy of consideration. One easy solution to the immediate problem of an absence of coverage is perhaps to abandon the medium of the nineteenth century and to go for the medium of the twenty-first. If, as Jack Straw maintained, one had to take note of the increasing price of *Hansard* and alongside the death of the parliamentary report the public was being excluded from political communication, then one answer would be to make electronic versions of parliamentary documentation more easily available through the Internet. In this way, the passing of a type of newspaper need not be mourned since the Internet could provide an even better alternative, as could dedicated parliamentary television channels. To quote Taras again:

> The old news is not about to disappear. The old structures remain very much in place. But the new news that is arising alongside the old has the capacity to change the equation in important ways. The geological plates of media-political relations may be about to shift … journalists may lose some of their power, while politicians may regain some of theirs. (1996: 7)

Taras may be overstating the case and conflating access to media with communication but he is, nonetheless, pointing out something important, namely, that out of this decline there is a possibility of positive change. His comments apply to the Canadian parliament but they should have a wider resonance and they raise the question of reform of institutions for an age of global and multi-media communication where institutionalized politics is no longer the only form of legitimate political activity.

Chapter 5

British newspaper coverage of parliament and politics

If the argument in the previous chapters has been that there has been a change in the pattern of political and parliamentary coverage and that the change has been, in the main, for the worse, the next few chapters will attempt to substantiate the various claims made by concerned writers. This chapter focuses on an analysis of political and parliamentary coverage in British newspapers, while the following chapters will focus on other media and on French and German newspapers. The chapter is divided into three main sections. The first gives an overview of the data based on an analysis of the political and parliamentary items coded and illustrates the pattern of change across newspapers as a whole. The second section provides a more detailed assessment of how the changes have affected the presence of parliament in the British print media. The final section examines how the changed pattern of parliamentary and political coverage has impacted on the chances of Members of Parliament appearing in print.

Throughout this chapter, and the following chapters, the data will be presented in both table and diagrammatic form. More detailed data can also be found in an Appendix of Tables: these are not included in the main body of the text since they only supplement the narrative provided here.

Overview of data

Four different categories of newspaper items were coded as a way of trying to identify whether or not there had been a change in the coverage of politics and of parliamentary institutions. The four categories – described in Chapter 3 (see pp. 21–23) – were:

- primary political items;
- secondary political items;
- parliamentary items;
- European political items.

These four categories would encompass all the ways in which political actors were represented in newspapers, with particular attention also being paid to the location of their appearance.

The total number of all four categories of items coded from the sample of 15 issues of each of three newspapers is set out in Table 5.1. This table highlights one of the ways in which the *Financial Times* differs from the other two newspapers: it showed an increase in the total number of items coded, while the others showed a significant decrease.

Table 5.1: Total number of items coded, three British newspapers

	1986	1996	% change
Financial Times	210	273	+30
Guardian	383	279	−27
Daily Telegraph	347	265	−24

Such overall figures hide important changes in the distribution of the coded items across the three newspapers. Since all the items were coded according to four categories, it is possible to compare changes within each of the categories. Figure 5.1 and Table 5.2 set out the relevant data.

Figure 5.1 and Table 5.2 show that:

- For the *Guardian* and the *Daily Telegraph*, the number of primary political items coded had decreased and the category of parliamentary items had disappeared by 1996. This altered the overall pattern of coverage: the *Guardian* carried 65 parliamentary page items in the 1986 sample, the *Telegraph* 59. The effect of these two changes dramatically reduced the number of items of a primarily political character in these two newspapers.
- For the *Financial Times*, both the number of primary political items and the number of secondary political items increased. Moreover, since it did not have a dedicated parliamentary page in 1986, there was no change of the sort identified for the other two newspapers.

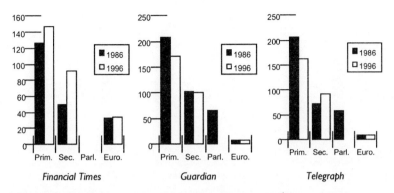

Figure 5.1: Political items in three newspapers, 1986 and 1996: primary, secondary, parliamentary and European

Table 5.2: Distribution of all coded items across four categories*

	Primary items		Secondary items		Parliamentary items		European items		Total
	No.	%	No.	%	No.	%	No.	%	
FT 1986	127	60	50	24	–		33	16	210
FT 1996	147	54	92	34	–		34	12	273
Guardian 1986	208	54	102	27	65	17	8	2	383
Guardian 1996	171	61	101	36	–		7	3	279
Telegraph 1986	206	59	73	21	59	17	9	3	347
Telegraph 1996	163	62	92	35	–		10	4	265

* In this, and other tables, figures have been rounded up or down so that percentages do not always total 100%.

To find out more precisely what sorts of items were lost, it is necessary to explore both the changing nature of the newspaper and its changing priorities. One gets a sense of the former by looking at differences in the way the 1996 newspaper was organized, relative to its predecessor, with regard to the distribution of physical space as between text, headlines and photographs. These are shown in Figure 5.2, which, like most others in this section, deals with primary and parliamentary items only; secondary political items have been excluded on the grounds that political actors play only a minor role in secondary items and so do not reflect how political items should be covered, or should be covered

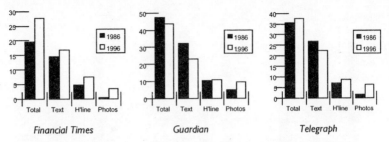

Note: *FT* n [or total cases] = 127 in 1986; n = 147 in 1996; *Guardian* 273 and 171 respectively; *Telegraph* 262 and 163 respectively.

Figure 5.2: Total size of items by text, headline and photo space, all primary and parliamentary items ('000 cm. sq.)

when seen from a political actor's own point of view. European items have also been excluded because they normally make no reference to British domestic political actors.

Figure 5.2 points to a number of interesting changes in newspapers between 1986 and 1996:

- Although the number of items coded for both the *Telegraph* and the *Guardian* declined – from 262 to 163 and from 273 to 171 respectively – the total amount of space devoted to the coded items either increased slightly or decreased slightly. This can be explained by the large *decrease* in the text space taken up by the coded items and the large *increase* in the space taken up by headlines and photos. This can also be seen in Figure 5.3.
- Photos and headlines take up more space in 1996 than in 1986. To give one specific example: in 1986 the *Telegraph* devoted 1,637 cm. sq. to photos compared with 6,257 cm. sq. in 1996.
- The change for the *Financial Times* differs from that for the other two newspapers. The increase in the number of coded items is accompanied by an increase in the use of text, larger headlines and more photos. The increase in the photo space taken up by these items is quite marked.
- In all three cases, the average space taken up by an individual item in 1996 is greater than it was in 1986, though as Figure 5.2 suggests, this may be due to larger headlines and more photographs.

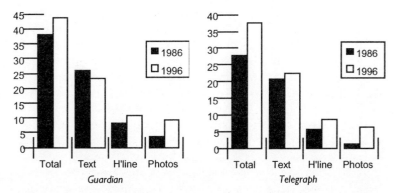

Note: Guardian n = 208 in 1986 and n =171 in 1996; *Telegraph* n = 206 in 1986 and n = 171 in 1996.

Figure 5.3: Distribution of space in two newspapers, primary political items only ('000 cm. sq.)

The disappearance of the parliamentary page items (see Figure 5.1 and Table 5.2) has clearly had a dramatic impact on the number of items coded for two out of the three newspapers, and this has also had an impact on the distribution of space given over to items. For example, it has reduced the amount of space devoted to text, a style of coverage which was more common to the parliamentary page items. In fact, as Figure 5.3 shows, it has left two out of the three newspapers carrying fewer primary political items but taking up more space in 1996 than in 1986. (See Figure 5.1 for the *Financial Times*.)

The redistribution of space within the newspapers examined – redistribution with respect to the relationship between text space, headline space and photo space – questions the assumption that larger newspapers automatically translate into more items and more text, or, in this particular case, that more space devoted to all the items means more items and more text. One can begin to appreciate the complexity of this point by exploring some specific items in a little detail.

If one takes the *Guardian* as an example – and it is perhaps the paper which has travelled furthest in design and layout terms – one finds that in 1986 the most common (modal) size of a primary political news item was 86 cm. sq.,whereas in 1996 it was 98 cm. sq. The median figure is also higher for 1996 – 128 cm. sq. – as compared with 106 cm. sq. in 1986. The same pattern is true for the other two newspapers. This suggests that the typical items carried in 1996 occupy, on the whole, more physical space than their equivalents in 1986. In other words, there are fewer items in 1996 but each of the 1996 items is likely to be larger than its 1986 predecessor. What has been lost are many of the small items of text which were in evidence in 1986 and before the newspapers redesigned themselves into a more visually attractive medium.

One can see this from another perspective. In 1986, 25% (or 52 items) of the *Guardian*'s primary political items were made up of text which took up 74 cm. sq. of space or less. In 1996, only 18% (or 31 items) were of that size or under. In the case of the *Telegraph*, the respective figures are 25% (52 items) of items taking up 56 cm. sq. of text space or less in 1986, with only 14% (23 items) of items occupying that space or less in 1996. For the *Financial Times*, a quarter of items took up 72 cm. sq. or under, a figure not very different from that of 1996 where 28.6% of items had text occupying 70 cm. sq. or less. In this respect, the *Financial Times* is once again different from the other two newspapers analysed.

A related point which also needs to be borne in mind is that the newspaper in 1996 is different in design and structure from its predecessor in 1986, for instance in the different width of columns, font sizes and so on. This, too, can have an impact of sorts. It suggests, therefore, that comparisons of newspapers across time should not assume that the overall space is used in identical ways, or, more simply, that a square centimetre of text in 1996 is identical to one in 1986. It could be argued, as one journalist did, that the loss of the shorter piece or item may not be such a critical loss after all since such items provided the minimum of information and no explanation or contextualization of what is referred to. Such an argument may be valid up to a point but it does not address the real cause of concern that *any* loss whatsoever is a *reduction* of a particular type of information and so can be significant in itself.

The change in the nature of the coverage can also be seen in the use of photographs and headlines. In both cases, and for all three newspapers, there were more and larger photographs used in 1996 than in 1986, and the headlines were, on average, larger in 1996 than in 1986. To re-emphasize the point a little: in the *Guardian* in 1986, headlines represented some 22% of total space; in 1996, that figure stood at some 24%. For photos, the difference is starker: in 1986, they took up 9% of total space but this figure had risen to 24% in 1996. For the *Telegraph*, photos took up 20% of space in 1996, but only 5% of space in 1986. (See Tables A1a–c in Appendix 2. Tables in the Appendix add more detail to the data provided here.)

All this goes to suggest that what one is looking at is not only change in the coverage of politics and parliamentary institutions but parallel change in the nature of newspapers themselves.

Secondary political items and items about the European Community/ Union

Are these patterns of change also true for secondary political items? Secondary political items also permit political actors to appear in newsprint, albeit in a more limited capacity. In addition, however, they also broaden the political agenda and allow one to glimpse other definitions of what is or is not political, institutionally or otherwise. For example, an item about education reform might discuss changes going on in schools and in the last paragraph might quote the Secretary of State for Education. Such an item is not a parliamentary item in the institutional sense of the phrase but it does involve political actors. Nor is it a primary political item inasmuch as a political actor is not an active and central figure in the story. It could be argued that as governments have broadened their involvement in areas of public and private life, items such as this are likely to increase: at each step of the way, the media now want to know what governments/ministers/MPs will do about this or that concern or incident.

It is therefore possible that, as the institutionally based political item disappears, a different type of political item comes to the fore: political actors may emerge in other contexts as parliament itself undergoes changes and allegedly loses its strong appeal for MPs and journalists alike. If that sort of change is taking place, it offers up the possibility that the range of items has expanded to pull in other actors and to engage politicians in a much broadened agenda. However, as Table 5.2 above indicates, the number of European items coded has hardly changed at all for any of the three newspapers but the change in the number of secondary political items has been more dramatic for both the *Financial Times* (50 items in 1986 to 92 items in 1996) and the *Telegraph* (73 to 92 respectively). The *Guardian*'s share of secondary items remains more or less constant. This change could partly be explained by the former two newspapers seeking to broaden their appeal by including a range of items which would not have been used in the past. Once again, part of the explanation of the change which is taking place in the research reported here must lie in the changing nature of newspapers themselves. (For a more detailed comparison of European political coverage in the press, see pp. 55–56 below.)

Detailed analysis of items

Subjects and categories

All the coded items were analysed in detail. Each item was coded by type, subject, location of the item, the focus, where it was set, how much comprised direct quotes and so on.

In terms of broad descriptions or categories – was a primary political item, for instance, a 'political, social and economic' (pse) item, or an item about Northern Ireland, or a foreign news item? – there is little that distinguishes the year 1986 from 1996. The largest category for both years and for all three newspapers was the broad political, social and economic category: over 70% of all items. In the case of the *Telegraph*, these items accounted for 83% of all items in 1986 but for only 71% in 1996. In the case of the other two newspapers, the figures varied within the narrow range of 73–77%. Generally speaking, with the above *Telegraph* figure and foreign news (see below) excepted, there is a certain degree of constancy in the distribution of items across these broad categories. As regards news items about individual countries and their relations with Britain, there is a recorded decrease between 1986 and 1996 for all three newspapers. (For more details, see Appendix Tables A2a–c.) This may be specific to the sample days in 1986 as it covered the period of antagonism between Libya and the United States and Britain.

The more interesting difference between the years is to be found in the secondary political items categories. Despite the number of such items increasing or remaining at a high level (for example, for the *Guardian*), fewer of them fall in the general political, social and economic category in 1996 than in 1986, and more fall into the 'other' category. This suggests that political actors are now appearing in an incidental and secondary capacity in a whole range of different items and considerably more than they did in 1986.

How well was the European Community/European Union covered by the press in these primary and parliamentary items? There is an increase in the number of items dealing with the EC/EU and Britain recorded in 1996 compared with 1986 – from five to 12 items in the case of the *Guardian* and from eight to nine in the case of the *Telegraph*.

This level of coverage, however, does not comprise all the coverage given to EC/EU affairs since, as noted earlier, these are items in which the EC/EU features but in which no British political actor does. In simple terms, these would be items about European Community/Union affairs *per se*. Table 5.2 and Figure 5.1 nonetheless indicate how little coverage

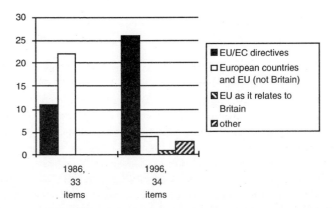

Figure 5.4: Items focused on the EC/EU in the *Financial Times*

of that nature can be found in two of the three newspapers in our sample, the exception being the *Financial Times* whose coverage is substantial (33 items in 1986, 34 in 1996) and includes several aspects of the European Community/Union (Figure 5.4).

One explanation for this pattern of coverage across the three newspapers would be that the *Financial Times* has a more specific business- and Europe-oriented readership which demands information and news about matters or issues affecting European business and finance. By contrast, the other papers are more domestic in orientation with a more widespread readership across the socio-economic spectrum. Overall, coverage of EU matters is not particularly intense in British newspapers, though this would probably also be true across Europe with wide variations in evidence from one year to another. Fundesco's analysis of *The European Union in the Media 1996* (1997) observed that there was 'a decrease of 17.1%' in the total number of 'informative and evaluative texts bearing some relation to the European Union'. While some European newspapers did have a satisfactory amount of coverage (defined as '300 units of text in any six-week period'), the *Guardian* had the third lowest strike rate (55 items) and the *Times* the lowest (43). One other newspaper coming into the low category was the *Frankfurter Allgemeine Zeitung* (92 units) which features later on in this report (1997: 33). Other newspapers such as *Le Monde* and *Le Figaro*, also featured in this study, show a decline between 1995 and 1996. What must be added, though, is that the average number of units published per month in 1994, 1995 and 1996 is, on the whole, greater than the average figures for 1992. For example, the *Frankfurter Allgemeine Zeitung* had an average of 82 units in 1992, but 181 and 176 in 1994 and 1995 respectively, coming down to 66 in 1996 (Fundesco, 1997: 73).

Our data also reflect a change in the pattern of coverage over time. Although Table 5.2 and Figure 5.1 inidicate that there are few items in two of the three British papers that are exclusively about European politics, this does not mean that the spectre of Europe was largely absent from the collected data. The European Commission/Union and the European Parliament featured in other items as well as in a number of different ways. The European Commission could, for instance, be part of a controversy on matters of trade or finance (or indeed BSE!). In this and other ways, the European political dimension did feature in the British, as in other, news media.

Looking at the whole question of European political coverage in the media from this perspective offers a much broader outlook than simply identifying items which were exclusively about European issues. The data reveal some interesting comparisons. In 1986, the *Telegraph*, for example, carried 17 items (out of a total of 347 items, or 5%) whose main subject matter was EU affairs, broadly defined. The figure for 1996 was 46 (or 17% of all 1996 items). The *Guardian* also had 17 items in 1986 (or 4%) but only 22 (8%) in 1996, while the *Financial Times* had 45 such items (or 21%) in 1986 and 52 in 1996 (or 19%). The German papers were akin to the *Telegraph*: the *Frankfurter Allgemeine Zeitung* (*FAZ*) figures were 20 and 46 (9% and 15% respectively) across the decade and the *Süddeutsche Zeitung* (*SDZ*) 34 and 53 (9% and 16% respectively). There are no comparable data for the French papers in 1986 but in 1996 *Le Monde* carried 40 items, *Le Figaro* 29 and *Libération* 19.

More interesting than this set of figures are data relating to the location of these items – that is, how many of them were actually set in a European location, in the Commission, Brussels or the European Parliament. Although none of the papers investigated carried more than *three* items which were located in the European Parliament for more than 50% of their content, for all the newspapers bar the *Financial Times* and the *FAZ*, the Commission/Brussels was a major location – that is, more than 50% of the content was located in that particular setting – in a range of between seven items (*SDZ*) and 14 items (*Telegraph*) in 1986. In 1996, the range was between 10 and 17 (for example, for *Le Figaro*). Exceptionally, the *FAZ* had no such items located in the Commission/Brussels in 1986. The *Financial Times* is worth separating from the others because its coverage is consistently high in this area: 18 items in

1986 and 21 in 1996. Here again, the British press sits quite comfortably among its European rivals.

More specific subject categories, too, have remained broadly unchanged even though the absolute number of primary political items coded decreased for two of the three newspapers (see Appendix Tables A3a–c). There are, perhaps inevitably, some exceptions to this. These include:

- A larger number of general political items and fewer economic policy items in 1996 compared with 1986 for all three newspapers. This could be reflecting a broadening out of the news agenda, with newspapers covering general political stories – for instance, dissent, conflict, disputes – more than just specific policy matters or issues. One can see this in the case of the *Financial Times* where general political items increased from 6% to 18% and economic policy items decreased from 29% to 16%.

- The appearance of many specific time-bound items such as the Westland affair in 1986, which involved internal political upheaval within the Conservative government. One senior minister (Michael Heseltine) resigned after a Cabinet row over whether or not a European consortium should take over the Westland helicopter company in preference to an American buyer. The affair snowballed and was to engulf other ministers and their officials, as allegations flew back and forth about the release of confidential letters and general political skulduggery. Part of the episode could, with hindsight, be considered as a variant of the 'sleaze' story since reputations were at stake and malpractice in government by ministers and advisers was at the centre of many of the commentaries at the time. In 1996, there was concern over BSE in cattle, a topic absent from the 1986 analysis.

- As for specifically 'sleaze' items, that is items concerning financial or political impropriety generally, the data are perhaps unrevealing. The key categories in 1996 related to the sale of military arms to Iraq and, more particularly, the Scott Inquiry into such sales of arms, and a more general category of sleaze comprising misconduct on the part of government or individual MPs. A total of 11 such items were coded for the *Financial Times* in 1996, 12 for the *Guardian* and eight for the *Telegraph* (7%, 7% and 5% respectively). The figures for 1986 are lower – two, two and five items respectively – though it is important to note that some such items were possibly included in the 'Westland' category rather than as separate sleaze items. In the German sample, scandal items accounted for 2% of items for the *SDZ* in 1986 and 1%

in 1996, and 1% and 2% for the *FAZ* in 1986 and 1996 respectively. Generally speaking, it is difficult to conclude from this that the British press is more interested in such items than any of the other newspapers sampled.

• A general decline in the number of items about, or involving, local government in Britain. Again, one needs to note that in 1986, the national Labour Party was at loggerheads with the radical political group Militant, and with a group of Liverpool councillors.

The significance of the *absolute decline* in the number of primary items coded is perhaps masked by the fact that the above discussion is based on percentages and fairly broad subject categories. What is overlooked in such an analysis is the extent to which the *thinning out* of items impacts on the range and diversity of subject matter *within* the subject categories. By examining in a little detail the implications of the loss of the parliamentary page items, one can see the impact of thinning out.

Parliamentary items, it should be recalled, generally dealt with debates and events taking place within the House of Commons and more specifically within the chamber itself. Sometimes, as is common today (as in 1996), these debates and events find their way onto the front or other pages of the newspaper. In 1986, they could make two appearances: once in their own right on the parliamentary page, and once as items worthy of, say, a front-page lead (or vice versa). More often than not, they would simply appear in their own right on the parliamentary page.

In a separate analysis of the collected data, all the items appearing on the parliamentary page on five separate days were examined in detail for both the *Telegraph* and the *Guardian*. Of the 36 items which appeared on these pages in the *Telegraph*, only six (17%) were also mentioned on other pages. For the *Guardian*, 28 items appeared on the parliamentary page with nine (32%) also mentioned on other pages.

What were the items reported on the parliamentary page but *not* considered worthy of a mention elsewhere? The list is extensive and includes the sale of British Gas, navy contracts, aid for refugees, the opium crop, violence at News International's new printing plant at Wapping, changes to the Housing Bill, the sale of London's County Hall, the tercentenary of parliament, a green paper on health care, and so on. This list shows very clearly the impact of the loss of the parliamentary page in terms of the narrowing of the range of items which emerge in the press out of the parliamentary arena. As Straw (1993) also argued in his paper, contemporary press coverage does not well reflect the *diversity* of subject matter

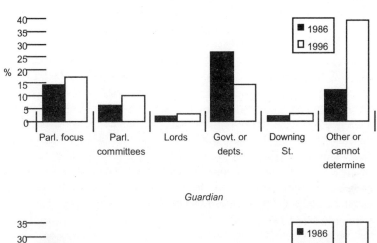

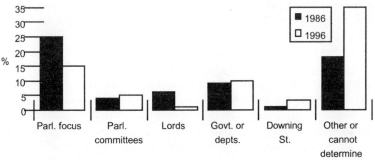

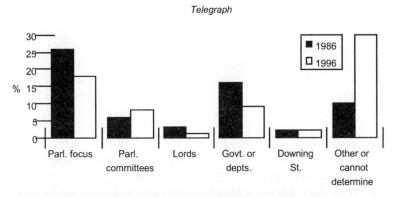

Figure 5.5: Percentage of items located in five main political locations (all primary and parliamentary items coded)

considered in parliament. This example, albeit drawn from a limited analysis, lends his position some support.

The location of coded items

Is it possible to determine whether or not a shift has taken place in the types of items published and whether in 1996 more attention is paid to politics outside parliament than within it? One way of doing this is to look at the main locations of an item. Figure 5.5 and Table A4 set out the main political locations of primary and parliamentary items drawn from the sample and emphasize the impact of the loss of the parliamentary page items for both the *Guardian* and the *Telegraph*.

There are two obvious points to make here. The first is that as the number of items specifically located in all five parliamentary or governmental settings declines, the number of items located *outside* these settings increases. Why this should be so is not obvious: one possibility is that ministers and MPs are more active in some way outside the main settings identified. Another possibility is that what they do outside those settings is more newsworthy. The second point is that by 1996, there was less coverage of governmental reports, departmental announcements and related items. This is quite possibly a direct consequence of the thinning out of items across the board.

Significantly, though, in a number of items in the 1996 sample, it was difficult to identify the precise location of an item: there was no statement, no indication or clue specific enough to point to the location. This sometimes happened in cases where the item was about parliament in some way but where there was no real way of identifying the location. Items about House of Commons committee reports could be of this nature. If they start with a sentence such as 'A report by an all-party group of MPs says that ...', a reader has no clues as to where the action takes place. Many such items simply refer to 'a report' with no real sense of the item being located anywhere in particular. As was discussed above, this question of physical location is significant for considering concerns expressed about the decline in parliamentary coverage.

The parliamentary page items

The consequences of the loss of the parliamentary page items has already been commented upon. Given their importance for this research, it is worthwhile pursuing this a little further. The dedicated space allocated to parliamentary affairs varied from about one half of a broadsheet page (in the case of both the *Telegraph* and the *Guardian)* to a full page (as was

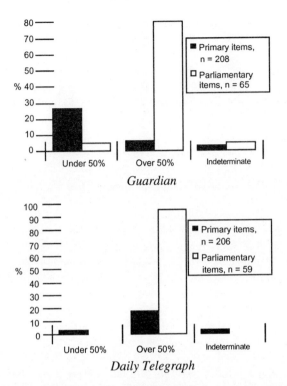

Figure 5.6: Percentage of the contents of items located in parliament – a comparison of primary and parliamentary items in 1986

usually the case with *The Times*). This space would carry reports of activities in parliament. In the main, these would be reports of debates but there were also items relating to the introduction of bills, and such like. Inevitably, not all that took place in parliament on particular days was carried in that dedicated space but at least a selection of material was being made available. And, as has already been described, it was a selection of both newsworthy and less newsworthy items.

Although not all the parliamentary page items were primarily located in and around parliament, most were. This is especially so for the *Guardian* since its page was not as neatly cut off as the *Telegraph*'s 'Yesterday in Parliament' page and occasionally other items would intrude. Nonetheless, 82% of its items were primarily set in the House; for the *Telegraph*, the figure was 98%. More importantly, such items were

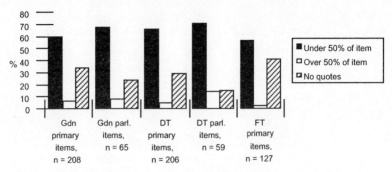

Figure 5.7: Percentage of item consisting of direct quotes, 1986

predominantly about what was going on *in* parliament, rather than else-where (Figure 5.6).

The difference between the primary items and those on the parliamentary page is stark. The significance of the decreased interest in what is going on in the House as a physical location can be seen in some other data. Whereas in 1986, 87 (32%) of all the *Guardian*'s primary political and parliamentary items were located in parliament for over 50% of their content, that is, were mainly about things happening in parliament, the figure for 1996 is only 38 (22%). The respective percentage figures for the *Telegraph* are 34% in 1986 and 17% in 1996 (see also Table A5). The disappearance of the dedicated space has thus had a crucial effect on how many items about parliament appear in the sampled newspapers. However, few of the parliamentary page items consisted wholly of verbatim extracts from speeches. Much of their content comprised accounts, in the third person, of what had been said. It was less of a version of *Hansard* than might at first have been assumed (Figure 5.7).

By 1996, although fewer items had no direct quotes at all, there were also fewer in which quotes made up over 50% of the item. In effect, by 1996 nearly 80% of all sampled primary and parliamentary items used direct quotes sparingly; that is, they made up less than half the item. The comparable figure for 1986 was considerably lower (ranging from 57 to 71%) (see Tables A6a–b). This suggests that a more interpretative style of reporting is now common, though more conclusive evidence for this must await a separate study on this specific theme.

Perhaps the biggest, and the most critical, change which has come about as a result of the demise of the parliamentary page is the reduction in the opportunities for publicity offered to Members of Parliament. As the next section will show, the parliamentary items page offered MPs a good opportunity to be seen and heard by the public, more so than was possible in the primary political items.

Political actors in newspapers
The changes which have taken place in the coverage of parliament and of politics have had an impact on the chances of MPs making an appearance in the print media. As this section will show, with fewer parliamentary and political items in newspapers, fewer MPs get mentioned.

To arrive at such conclusions, one has first to discover how MPs are reported in news items. To do this, each individual actor mentioned in an item was coded (up to a maximum of 15 individual actors) in the order in which they appeared. Sometimes, such actors would be collectivities in the sense that journalists often refer to 'the government' or to a department as an actor, but more often than not the actors were individuals drawn from across the political scene. For each item, then, it becomes possible to list all the actors referred to and whether they are quoted directly, indirectly, a combination of both or simply referred to in passing. This procedure establishes some sort of hierarchy of prominence and access and can be used to assess who is or is not seen as newsworthy or important enough to quote directly.

Inevitably, with up to 15 actor positions available for each item, the total potential number of actors which can occupy each and every one of these positions is immense. In practice, the register of actors is clearly more limited, though still large. For both the 1986 sample and the 1996 sample, some 900 separate actors were coded. Sometimes, the distinction between one actor and the next was not as clear-cut as perhaps it could have been. Journalists, for example, use shorthand to describe different groupings of actors – 'Tory grandees', 'senior Tories', 'Tory strategists' – terms which, to the lay person, probably signify little. Are these one and the same? There really is no way of knowing.

Although efforts were made to distinguish between such groupings, the way in which the figures below are calculated tends to combine similar elements. Thus, 'Tory MPs' can be grouped together with 'Tory back-benchers', 'ministers' with 'senior ministers', and so on. This method of grouping also provides a useful, albeit crude, way to explore the balance of representation as between the political parties. As will become evident, the balance of reporting is very firmly in a government's favour and, in the British political system where the majority party *is* the government, in the majority party's favour. This is not surprising:

governments act, and those actions often lead news items, while oppositions react.

Figure 5.8 is based on data derived from examining the number of
appearances of the first *three* mentioned *political* actors only, grouped
into political parties. (Table A7 provides an analysis of the first seven
mentioned actors; beyond that references to political actors tail off quite
rapidly.) Two points about Figure 5.8 are important to remember. First,
the general categories – from the opposition to party advisers – are not
included in the categories in the figure: only *named* political actors are
taken into account. There are two exceptions: first, a figure for the
number of times the government as an actor is mentioned is included;
second, but very rarely, ministers who may have a governmental role but
who are not MPs are included in the list, for example, Lord Young at the
Department of Trade and Industry in 1986. The second point is that the
number of items analysed in 1986 is much larger than the number of
items dealt with a decade later. The 1986 analysis of primary and parliamentary page items took account of 665 items; the figure for 1996 is 481.
This difference – a 28% decrease – is bound to have some important
effects on the way political actors are represented, which will become
clearer as the data are analysed.

The first set of columns represents the number of times that the speci-
fied categories of actors were mentioned in the total sample of items. So,
for example, in the case of the *Financial Times*, the figure for 1986 shows
that the government was the first mentioned political actor in 39 items
(out of a total of 127), the Conservatives as a group in 22, and Labour in
two. The difference between all these mentions – 63 – and the total of 127
possible first mentions is made up by references to other actors, i.e. not
MPs.

Overall, the government and members of the governing party
dominate. There may be minor points of difference between the way
newspapers handle these two categories – for example, one can compare
the *Financial Times* in 1986 with the *Telegraph* in the same year – but
such differences may be due to variations in reporting style or choice of
items for each newspaper rather than more deep-seated reasons for
placing one category over another. The Labour Party and the third party,
be it a Liberal Alliance or Liberal Democrat Party, have a much lower
visibility at the beginning of news items. They get pulled into items later
down the ladder of importance (see also Appendix Table A7).

This type of analysis can also highlight the prominence of the prime
minister in British newspaper coverage of politics generally. The prime

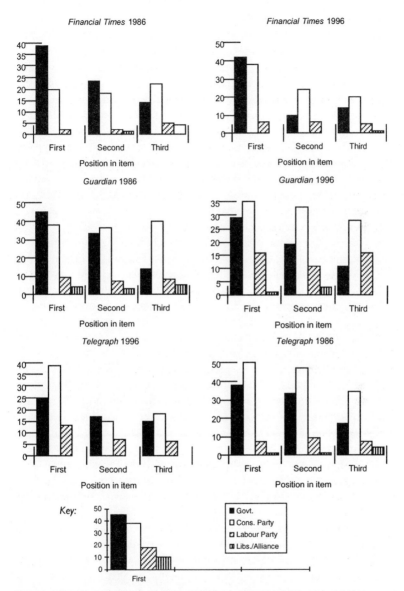

Figure 5.8: Number of mentions of named political actors in first three positions in primary political items, 1986

Note: 1986 totals: *Financial Times* 127 items, *Guardian* 208, *Telegraph* 206; 1996 totals: *Financial Times* 147; *Guardian* 171; *Telegraph* 163.

minister (Margaret Thatcher in 1986, John Major in 1996) is easily the most dominant figure; other Conservative politicians (home secretaries, foreign ministers, etc.) are mentioned but in no discernible order of prominence and much less frequently (see also Table A8 for 1986, Table A9 for 1996). That said, it is quite clear that politicians closest to the centre of political power are referred to most often. This is also the case for the other political parties, although there are few references to their members (see Table A10 for 1986, Table A11 for 1996). Lastly, in both years analysed, the respective prime ministers were mentioned more often than the opposition leaders. These sorts of findings lend support to some notion of a hierarchy of power and emphasize the way criteria of newsworthiness tend to militate against lesser MPs obtaining any significant coverage.

This emerges most clearly when exploring the impact of the disappearance of the parliamentary page on MPs' chances of getting themselves into print. In 1986, 65 items were coded on the *Guardian*'s parliamentary page (in reality more like half a page), and 59 in the *Telegraph*'s (the *Financial Times* had no dedicated space *per se* so it does not feature in this particular analysis). By separating those political actors appearing in primary political items from those appearing in items on the parliamentary page, one can get a sense of the breadth of the register of MPs making an appearance in newspaper items.

Table 5.3 sets out the distribution of MPs from the two main political parties in parliamentary and political items. It brings together an analysis of the number of Conservative and Labour MPs who are quoted either directly or indirectly, or both, in the first *ten* actors' positions – ten rather than seven or three so as to include as many MPs as possible in this analysis – in all the items coded. MPs from the other parties have been excluded partly on the grounds that they were hardly mentioned anyway.

Collapsing these figures a little, one finds that in 1986, 37 MPs or 30% (28 Conservative and nine Labour) out of a total of 123 MPs featured in the *Guardian*'s parliamentary page and *not* elsewhere in the paper. The *Telegraph*'s figures showed that 49 MPs or 41% (21 Conservative and 28 Labour) out of a total of 120 MPs appeared on the parliamentary page. For both newspapers, these are substantial figures; it is more important in the case of the *Telegraph* since the data show that there were more Labour MPs featured on the parliamentary page than elsewhere in the paper (36 as against 18). The total figure of Labour and Conservative MPs found in these two papers being awarded more than a simple mention or reference is thus 123 and 120 *out of a total complement of 650 or so MPs*!

Table 5.3: Number of Conservative and Labour MPs quoted in primary and parliamentary page items, ten positions, 1986

Guardian

	Primary political items, n = 208 (1)	*Parliamentary page items, n = 65 (2)*	*Number of MPs mentioned in (1) but not in in (2)*	*Number of MPs mentioned in (2) but not in (1)*	*Total MPs*
Conservative	53	52	29	28	81
Labour	33	18	24	9	42
Total	**86**	**70**	**53**	**37**	**123**

Telegraph

	Primary political items, n = 206 (1)	*Parliamentary page items, n = 59 (2)*	*Number of MPs mentioned in (1) but not in in (2)*	*Number of MPs mentioned in (2) but not in (1)*	*Total MPs*
Conservative	62	42	31	21	73
Labour	19	36	11	28	47
Total	**81**	**78**	**42**	**49**	**120**

Table 5.4: Number of Conservative and Labour MPs quoted in primary and parliamentary page items, ten positions, 1986 and 1996

	Financial Times		*Guardian*		*Telegraph*	
	Primary items, 1986 n = 127	*Primary items, 1996 n = 147*	*Primary and parliamentary, 1986 n = 273*	*Primary items, 1996 n = 171*	*Primary and parliamentary, 1986 n = 265*	*Primary items, 1996 n = 163*
Conservative	36	48	81	57	73	56
Labour	13	26	42	36	47	22
Total	**49**	**74**	**123**	**93**	**120**	**78**

Would as many MPs make an appearance without that dedicated parliamentary space? The data for 1996, compared with 1986, can be found in Table 5.4.

Table 5.4 shows quite clearly that with fewer primary political items in 1996 compared with 1986 *and* no parliamentary page, the overall number of different MPs making an appearance in the newspapers declines. In 1986, a total of 123 different MPs were given some direct access to the *Guardian*'s readers, and a total of 120 MPs to the *Telegraph*'s. By 1996, those figures had declined to 93 and 78 respectively. In both cases, the 1996 figures are not unlike the figures for MPs appearing in primary (and parliamentary) items alone in 1986 (70 for the *Guardian* and 78 for the *Telegraph*).

This is not the case for the *Financial Times*. There were more political items coded in 1996 than in 1986 (147 compared with 127) and so the number of parliamentary actors making an appearance on its pages is greater in 1996 than in 1986 (74 compared with 49) – though one has to remember that the 1986 figure is a particularly low one and reflects a newspaper which was much more finely tuned to a business and financial readership than the other two in the sample.

However one attempts to interpret these data, there is one overwhelming conclusion: the changing nature of two of the three newspapers in the sample – changes signalled by a reduction in political items of which the parliamentary page was clearly a part – has had a significant impact on the chances of the parliamentary contribution of MPs being made public through some of the major channels of political communication.

Chapter 6

British television news coverage of parliament

Television, unlike newspapers, offers a very different kind of medium for analysis. It does not have the tradition of the print media and its role within the political system is constantly changing, sometimes in radical ways. We can see this in the analysis presented here. In 1986, television cameras were still excluded from the Chamber of the House of Commons; it could not offer 'a window' on that particular world. This was not only in direct contrast with what was happening in other parliaments but it also contrasted with what was to take place after 1989 when television cameras first entered the chamber. Consequently, the two years analysed here represent different sets of practices and arrangements between the medium of television and parliament. One illustration of the significance of the change is that in 1986, it was not possible to show MPs speaking in the chamber: other means were used to connect MPs to their speeches such as using a photograph with text as a subtitle. By 1996, this practice had been abandoned as extracts from speeches in the chamber could be slotted in as appropriate.

By all accounts the television coverage of parliament has been generally considered a useful addition to the presentation of politics on television (see Blumler et al., 1990; Franklin, 1992; Ryle, 1991). Although there are criticisms of its coverage (see McDonald, 1994, for example), these are somewhat different from those voiced against the press. The press is often criticized for its interest in gossip and intrigue – an accusation perhaps less often directed at television given that it is a visual medium and usually requires those making statements to be seen on screen. This helps to explain the developing pattern of practices with respect to televising politics: the exclusion of cameras from the House and the need for faces on screen to explain and interpret the more formal nature of debates in the chamber may have encouraged the use of locations immediately outside parliament (for instance the public park known as College Green). Interviews conducted in these locations, even after television pictures were available from the House, allow for more focused and more succinct statements than would ever be possible from within the House itself. But for those advocating the televising of parliament, this was the sort of practice that undermined what was happening *in* the House. Better, in other words, to have sound and images from the House itself than a reflection of it on the outside.

Nevertheless, it is important not to forget that television coverage of parliament began less than a decade ago and that practices are constantly changing even within the context of continued commitment to political coverage. The creation of Millbank, about 100 yards from Westminster, as a centre of much political coverage can still go hand-in-hand with a diminution of the importance of political programming culled directly from the House. As Hill (1993) has pointed out, both the *Yesterday in Parliament* and *Today in Parliament* programmes on BBC Radio 4 have suffered reductions in allotted times in recent years and are now broadcast on the long-wave frequency only. Such programmes may continue to be reassessed.

That there have been other changes in the coverage of politics and parliamentary institutions in the ten years between 1986 and 1996 will emerge in the analysis provided in the following sections. However, these changes should be seen in the context of a continually evolving relationship between political actors and television journalists, as well as in the context of a changing relationship between print and broadcast media.

Overview of data

The sample for the analysis of television news content consists of two weeks (Monday to Friday) of the main terrestrial television news programmes. These are BBC1's *Nine O'Clock News* (9.00 pm), ITN's *News at Ten* (10.00 pm) and Channel 4's *Channel Four News* (7.00 pm). Each week was drawn from a different month in both 1986 and 1996. The decision to analyse two periods of five consecutive days, as opposed to rolling weeks, was influenced by the difficulty of acquiring complete news programmes from 1986. In the event, a total of 28 news bulletins was successfully recorded for the analysis. Two bulletins were missed: one from the 1986 sample (BBC1 9.00 pm) and one from the 1996 sample (ITN 10.00 pm). Later sections of this chapter will also refer to detailed analysis of news coverage on Sky Television and an analysis of regional television news (BBC's *Midlands Today* and ITV's *Central News*). The following sections, however, focus entirely on the three main national services: BBC1, ITN and Channel 4.

In both years, the length of the news programmes was similar (BBC1 and ITN with approximately 25 minutes and Channel 4 with approximately 50 minutes), and variations were slight and insignificant. Television news programmes present their own problems when it comes to analysing their content. Prominent stories are often made up of two or three separate and distinct journalistic packages which, for quantitative purposes, could be taken to represent different items. A good example of this in 1996 was the coverage of the British beef crisis. During the research period this crisis dominated a large percentage of the 1996 news time and very often the subject would be treated from a number of different angles or would highlight different but related problems. A news programme would, for example, headline its report with the beef crisis and then explore, say, the health risk of eating beef, and then the economic crisis affecting British farmers. When such a news story was recorded, its component parts would be taken to represent different items. Thus, in the case mentioned here, one would list two different items both of which dealt with the beef crisis. A new location to the story or a different reporter/interviewee were taken as indicators of a change in the angle of the story. Such a practice might suggest that there were more items than story subjects, something which is obviously not the case. The alternative practice of counting the subject as the item – for example, beef crisis – would have had the opposite effect of suggesting that news programmes covered very few items.

As with the analysis of British newspapers, a distinction was made between items in which political actors played a significant, prominent or leading role (primary items) and items in which they played a minor, secondary, or insignificant one (secondary items). In contrast to the analysis of the press, though, it is not possible to create a category of parliamentary items. Television news, in this respect, is structured differently. Table 6.1 identifies the total number of items featured in the three news programmes in the sample period. For the purposes of this research, an item's length was taken to include both the introduction by a newsreader or link person *and* the journalistic input or package itself.

Table 6.1: Total number of items featured in television news programmes (BBC, ITN, Channel 4) in 1986 and 1996

	1986	Total time (seconds)	1996	Total time (seconds)
Total number of items in sample	439		442	
Total number of primary items	111	**18,577**	94	**16,148**
Total number of secondary items	30	3,516	43	7,867
Total number of items with only a reference to political actors	4	–	6	–
Total time (in hours and mins)	–	**6hrs, 8 mins, 3 secs**	–	**8 hrs, 51 mins, 22 secs**

Note: 14 programmes in each year.

Between 1986 and 1996, the number of primary political items went down (by 15%) but the number of secondary items went up (by nearly 9%). The average length of each item also increased. Lastly, the total number of secondary items increased (from 30 in 1986 to 43 in 1996), suggesting that a subtle shift in emphasis took place, with 1996 news programmes including a higher number of items where political actors played a minor or secondary role. Table 6.2 identifies the changes in greater detail.

Given that the data relate to two years a decade apart, the subject matter of the coded items differs: in 1986 South Africa dominated the news, in 1996 Northern Ireland and the beef crisis dominated. The items, therefore, reflect the different eras in not unexpected ways. The prominence of the political items has changed across the years, albeit not very greatly, and this can be shown by calculating the number of primary

Table 6.2: Primary political news items in sample, 1986 and 1996

News programme	1986			1996		
	Items	Total time in secs	Average length	Items	Total time in secs	Average length
BBC1	34*	4,405	130	30	4,658	155
ITN	31	3,572	115	23*	3,113	135
Channel 4	46	10,580	230	41	8,377	204

*One news programme missing.

Table 6.3: Prominence of primary political items in three bulletins, 1986 and 1996

Sample period	1986				1996			
	9 days	*10 days*	*10 days*	*Total*	*10 days*	*9 days*	*10 days*	*Total*
Total primary political items	*BBC1* n = 34	*ITN* n = 31	*Cnl 4* n = 46		*BBC1* n = 30	*ITN* n = 23	*Cnl 4* n = 41	
As 1st item	5	5	8	18	6	4	6	16
As 2nd item	8	6	7	21	6	4	6	16
As 3rd item	2	5	6	13	2	2	6	10
Total items	**15**	**16**	**21**	**52**	**14**	**10**	**18**	**42**

political items which led the news programmes in the two different samples. Such a calculation could be said to be similar to the analysis of political items on the front pages of newspapers. In 1986, 52 items featured as either first, second or third item in the news bulletins' running orders, but only 42 did in 1996. Moreover, the drop in the number of items took place across all three channels (Table 6.3). (The 1986 BBC1 sample still had a larger number of items appearing in the first three positions than in 1996 even though there was one news bulletin less in the sample.)

Looked at from another perspective, in 1986 a total of 21 primary political items (out of a possible 30 items, that is ten days with three items per day) were featured as the first, second or third in *Channel Four News* bulletins' running order, but in 1996 only 18 featured in similar positions. The other channels show a similar pattern.

Political actors

If one defines prominence by the number of appearances made on television, then the most prominent political actor in 1986 was not the prime minister, Margaret Thatcher, but Geoffrey Howe, the foreign secretary. This is easily explained by reference to those items which featured in the sample. In 1986, the issue of the Commonwealth and South Africa was very prominent, and this propelled the foreign secretary into the news. He made 12 appearances as against Thatcher's seven and he was seen speaking on six occasions from a variety of settings. Thatcher was seen speaking only on four occasions from a variety of settings. Alongside these two political actors, a whole list of others can be

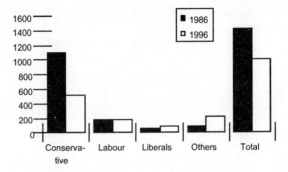

BBC1 *Nine O'Clock News*

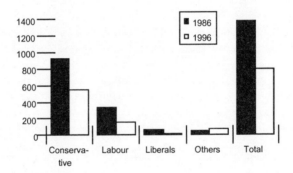

ITN *News at Ten*

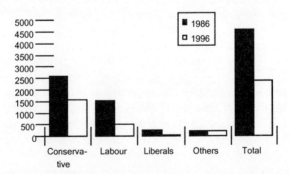

Channel 4 *Channel Four News*

Figure 6.1: Political actors 'seen and heard' in primary news items, by political party (excluding House of Lords) (seconds)

found. Some, such as the leader of the opposition, were prominent in parliament and politics, but many were in the news because they were dealing with a subject which was topical at the time. The likely pattern, then, is one of appearances dictated by considerations of newsworthiness rather than political status (though one cannot discount the latter affecting the former).

As there were no television cameras in the House in 1986, the ways in which political actors were represented differed greatly from the ways in which they can now be seen and heard from the House. In 1986, it was usual to show on screen a photo of the political actor in question and to relay sound extracts from the House. In this way, the photo and the voice would match. On this measure of prominence – how many times a particular actor was seen and heard from the House – Thatcher is seen and heard once but Howe is not. The point of this comparison is that the measure of prominence is complicated by the many ways in which actors could be represented. No one measure need necessarily outweigh another although in practice the number of times a political actor is simultaneously seen and heard is probably more significant than the number of times an actor is simply seen in the foreground or in the background. Figure 6.1 provides a general overview of the length of time for which party political actors were seen and heard, in primary news items.

The distribution of time according to political party may reflect particular news agendas. A heavy focus on Northern Ireland issues would inevitably increase the participation of Northern Ireland MPs and reduce that of MPs from the other political parties. Conversely, a story in which the government was heavily involved might increase the profile of government and ministers and lessen that of others. Nevertheless, the general pattern which emerges is one where political actors participate less often and less directly in news coverage. For instance, the total time actors were seen and heard across all the three channels in 1986 was 7,395 seconds (or 40% out of a total of 18,577 seconds for all the items), compared with 4,205 seconds in 1996 (or 26% out of a total of 16,148 seconds), and the decrease is in evidence across all three channels (see Table A12).

A number of conclusions can be drawn from this sort of data:

- The reduction in the number of long interviews now being used in news programmes is evident. In 1986 Channel 4 carried 12 lengthy interviews, that is of two minutes' duration and over, as part of its news coverage: a total of 1,992 seconds. In 1996, only four such interviews were coded and these took up 810 seconds.

- The decrease in the time taken up by political actors also impacts on the time taken up by political parties across the three channels. Labour Party actors were seen and heard for 2,032 seconds in 1986 but for only 862 seconds in 1996.
- The third political party is not, in practice, a third party. Indeed, in 1996, the group of Unionist MPs were given more access to the television screen than the members of the Liberal Democratic Party. This confirms the news-driven nature of coverage and the difficulty of a third party making inroads simply on the basis of its existence as such.

How prominent are key political actors in this distribution of seconds? Figure 6.2 contrasts the 'seen and heard' appearances of the prime minister with those of the leader of the opposition. The contrast between the two years can probably also be explained by the more prominent role that Tony Blair began to establish *vis-à-vis* John Major and other politicians by 1996.

If in 1986, political coverage was not a 'Maggie (Thatcher) and Neil (Kinnock)' affair – and the research surrounding the introduction of cameras into the House suggests that it was still not such an affair in the early 1990s (see Ryle, 1991) – by 1996, it would be difficult to support a similar conclusion. While the prime minister took up 15% of all time devoted to members of the Conservative Party on BBC1 in 1986, the corresponding figure for 1996 was 34%. The parallel figures for the

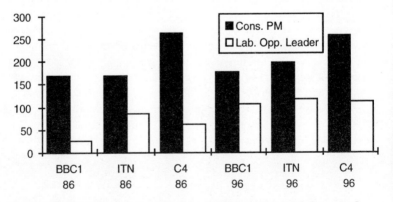

Figure 6.2: Number of seconds for which the prime minister and leader of the opposition were 'seen and heard' in 1986 and 1996

opposition leader on BBC1 are 15% and 60% (Table 6.4). That same pattern is repeated for the other two channels, suggesting that the leaders are becoming more, not less, prominent in television news coverage. Admittedly, the above figures take all appearances, including occasions when voices were used over photos, however fleeting or insignificant, into account; but comparing like for like it is difficult to avoid the conclusion that the leaders are more prominent as their lieutenants are pushed aside even further.

The pattern of change – and of decline – for the major parties can also be seen in Figure 6.3 which sets out the number of different political actors appearing in the news items, and in Figure 6.4, which shows the total number of times political actors from all the parties appeared in the bulletin. Thus, one figure counts *actors*, the other number of *appearances*.

Three final points need to be made concerning the overview of the data presented in this section. First, few political actors appear in secondary political items: eight in 30 items in 1986 and 19 in 43 items in 1996. This is not surprising because the nature of a secondary item means that political actors are not the main focus of the news story. However, in common with other findings, there is a slight increase in the number of secondary stories featuring political actors in 1996. This is particularly so for the government/Conservative Party actors and confirms their prominence in the overall news coverage. Secondly, the House of Lords features very rarely in any coverage: only three appearances by members of the

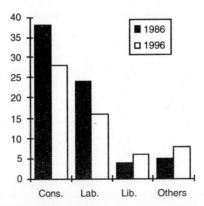

Figure 6.3: Number of different political actors appearing in primary news items, 1986 and 1996

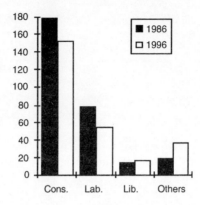

Figure 6.4: Total number of appearances by political actors from all parties in news items, 1986 and 1996

Lords were coded across both sample years. Finally, parliamentary committees also feature rarely. There was no coverage of committees in 1986, though this may not be surprising given that cameras were not allowed in House; they featured five times in the 1996 sample (for a total of 81 seconds!): three times on *Channel Four News* and once on each of the other channels.

Table 6.4: Time taken up by prime ministers and opposition leaders, primary items (seconds)

	1986			1996		
	BBC1*	ITN	Channel 4	BBC1	ITN*	Channel 4
Cons.	1,097	932	2,595	516	545	1,593
PM	169 (15%)	168 (18%)	263 (10%)	176 (34%)	197 (36%)	257 (16%)
Labour	184	331	1,517	180	158	524
Opposition Leader	28 (15%)	87 (26%)	63 (4%)	108 (60%)	120 (76%)	115 (22%)

*9 news programmes only.

Television news and parliament

From the television practitioner's point of view, the most dramatic change in the nature of political coverage over the decade of the analysis has undoubtedly been the introduction of television cameras into the House of Commons in 1989. Although by 1996 there appears to have been an overall decline in the number of appearances made by political actors and the duration of their appearances on the news programmes, the number of occasions on which actors are featured specifically in the chamber (as opposed to other locations) has increased and there has been an increase in the amount of time devoted to such actors speaking or being seen in the chamber. This should come as no surprise and, as will become clearer later on, it has prompted a change in the way coverage of politicians in and out of the House is now organized.

As with the analysis of newspapers, the research examined how political actors were seen on screen – whether as a photograph or speaking in the House, for example – and the location of the appearance. For 1986, a category of 'actor as voice-over' was used to code occasions when only an actor's voice could be heard. This was particularly pertinent for 1986 because of the nature of the television coverage of parliament. In contrast to the analysis of parliament in 1996, which included political actors both seen and 'seen and heard' in the chamber, in 1986 visual sketches of parliament or photographs of politicians were often used as a backdrop to extracts from speeches. Tables 6.5 and 6.6 illustrate the total number of items featuring audio or audio/visual reports from the chamber and the total number of seconds devoted to this footage. Overall, the total number of items including audio or audio/visual material from the chamber increased between 1986 and 1996 by 188% and within these items, the total number of seconds recorded in the chamber increased by 127%. The percentages indicate a dramatic increase in the time for which politicians are seen in the chamber and illustrate the importance of the introduction of television cameras for news producers.

Frequency of actors appearing in a location and the time taken up by each actor
The data for each of the political actors appearing in the news programme samples were examined in detail so as to provide information as to the location of the appearance and the nature of the appearance: whether the political actor was simply seen on screen, or 'seen and heard' from the chamber, and so on. In this way, it was possible to chart whether there has

Table 6.5: Television news coverage of parliament, 1986

	BBC1 n = 34	ITN n = 31	Channel 4 n = 46	**Total** **n = 111**
Number of items with audio or visuals	3	4	5	**12**
Number of seconds recorded in chamber	97*	99	253	**449**
Number of seconds of general pictures recorded in parliament	–	2 (from House of Lords)	–	**2**
Number of seconds of sound and pictures recorded in Lords	–	18	–	**18**

*12 seconds consisted of an audio extract over other politicians' images.

Table 6.6: Television news coverage of parliament, 1996; primary items*

	BBC1 n = 30	ITN n = 23	Channel 4 n = 41	**Total** **n = 94**
Number of items with audio or visuals	11	14	21	**46**
Number of seconds recorded in chamber	371	314	554	**1,239**
Number of seconds of general pictures recorded in chamber	99	105	66	**270**
Number of seconds of sounds and images recorded in Lords	10		22	**32**

*To this table one could add 55 seconds from committees in the House, and 6 seconds of images from the House of Lords.

been a change in the locations used and also whether there has been a change in the ways in which political actors make an appearance on screen. Overall, the data suggest that the number of appearances made by certain key politicians such as the prime minister, leader of the opposition, foreign secretary and so on remains fairly constant, although there are significant changes which can be attributed to the way different news items gain/lose prominence. In 1986, the foreign secretary made a large number of appearances because South Africa dominated the news, while in 1996, it was the home secretary who made many appearances. Such shifts in news agenda partly explain the changing prominence of political actors, although in both years analysed, the prime minister and the leader of the opposition are prominent. The leader of the third party is less so.

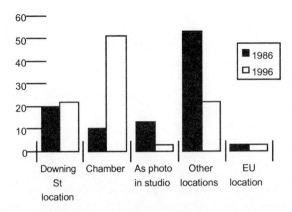

Note: 30 appearances in 1986, 37 in 1996.

Figure 6.5: Locations of appearances by the prime minister – percentage of all locations

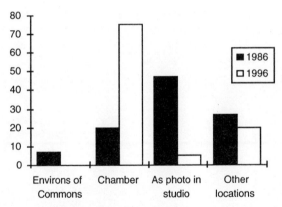

Note: 15 appearances in 1986, 20 in 1996.

Figure 6.6: Locations of appearances by the leader of the opposition – percentage of all locations

Perhaps more significant than this broad analysis of the data are data relating to the locations of appearances made by political actors. Figures 6.5 and 6.6 explore those data in relation to the prime minister and the leader of the opposition. (Tables A13 and A14 provide data for some other political figures.)

Despite the increase in the number of appearances made by these two political actors, particularly in the chamber, there has been a change in the locations in which other political actors are seen on screen. In 1996, the percentage of actors appearing in locations easily identifiable by the audience as political (for example, the Chamber in the House of Commons or Downing Street) had increased in comparison with 1986. By contrast, in 1996, the number of occasions on which political actors were seen in the television studio as a photograph or interviewed, or indeed seen in other locations, had declined in comparison with 1986. The Liberal leader, for instance, was seen only in the Commons in 1996, whereas in 1986 the leadership was seen in a number of other locations (Table A13). This greater attention to the institutional political arena provides the audience with a visual taste of the world inhabited by the politician, but it could also be argued that it offers a restricted register of workplaces. Other institutional locations are neglected – committees, departments, overseas, and so on. It is arguable, therefore, whether this concentration on the chamber is a positive thing.

Comparisons between the two years of the sample can also be made with respect to the length of time for which political actors were heard in the chamber and elsewhere. Figure 6.7 illustrates the extent to which the prime minister and leader of the opposition were 'seen and heard' or merely heard from the chamber.

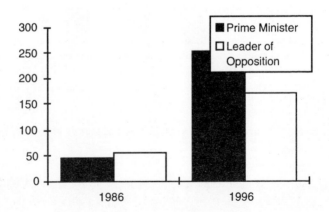

Figure 6.7: Total time key political actors 'heard' or 'seen and heard' from the chamber (seconds)

The difference between the pattern in 1986 and 1996 can be seen from another slightly different angle: in 1986 these two key political actors (and others) were making many *more* appearances *outside* the Chamber of the House. In 1986, the prime minister (Thatcher) was seen and 'seen and heard' outside the chamber for 579 seconds compared with John Major's 312 seconds in 1996. For the Labour Party leader the respective figures were 142 seconds and 77 seconds and for the leaders of the third party 290 seconds in 1986 and no time at all in 1996.

Many of these differences become apparent when one compares in a little more detail the pattern of coverage for two key political actors: the prime minister and the leader of the opposition (Tables 6.7 and 6.8). The concentration on the institutional setting is very clear.

The growing importance of the chamber as a source of sound and images is obvious. Whether this has had an effect on the length of extracts used from within the chamber is more difficult to say. Given that there were no cameras in the House in 1986, it is unlikely that news producers would have been particularly keen on carrying too many sound-only extracts in news items. Nonetheless, the average length of these sound-only extracts, surprisingly, did not differ greatly from the length of the sound and vision extracts from the House in 1996. For Margaret Thatcher, the average length of an extract was 15 seconds; for John Major, ten years later, it was also 15 seconds. For Neil Kinnock, the figure was 19 seconds, but for Tony Blair it was only 15 seconds. In this respect, then, access to visuals and sound from the House has translated into a greater use of such material.

Table 6.7: Appearances of Thatcher and Major, 1986 and 1996

	Thatcher, 1986	Major, 1996
Items appeared in	27	29
Seen for	305 secs	276 secs
Seen and heard outside chamber	263 secs	100 secs
Photo with newsreader's voice	23 secs	7 secs
Seen/seen and heard from chamber	45 secs	254 secs
Number of appearances	30 (inc. photo in studio)	37 (inc. photo in studio)
Heard in chamber	3 (of 30 times)	19 (out of 37)
In studio (as photo)	4 (out of 30))	1 (out of 37)
In and around Downing Street	6 (out of 30)	8 (out of 37)
Other location	16 (out of 30)	8 (out of 37)
European location	1 (out of 30)	1 (out of 37)

Table 6.8: Appearances of leaders of the Labour Party, 1986 and 1996

	Kinnock, 1986	Blair, 1996
Items appeared in	13	19
Seen for	57 secs	114 secs
Seen and heard for	27 secs	227 secs (of these 169 secs from the chamber)
Photo with newsreader's voice	58 secs	6 secs
Voice from chamber	56 secs	1 sec (with other image)
Number of different locations seen	15 (inc. photo in studio)	20 (inc. photo in studio)
Heard in chamber	3 (of 15 times)	15 (out of 20)
In studio (as photo)	7 (out of 15)	1 (out of 20)
Other location	5	4

For these two sets of actors, at least, the overall length of recorded extracts remained fairly constant. This is not the case when it comes to examining the use of all political actors' voices. Table 6.9 takes into account the number of seconds for which politicians were 'seen and heard' in all locations in 1996, but for 1986 the figures include the occasions when politicians' voices were used as extracts with photographs as a backdrop. In this way, one can argue, it is possible to work out how much time was given over directly to politicians' own voices.

Even if one allows for the odd missing second here and there in the calculations, the extent of the change appears quite dramatic. Overall, the amount of time taken up by all these primary items has decreased – from 18,577 seconds to 16,148 seconds – and the amount of time given directly to political actors has decreased from 4,322 seconds to 2,869 seconds. In percentage terms, political voices were heard for 23% of time taken up by primary political items in 1986 but only for 18% of the time taken up by the coded items in 1996. As regards how long these actors were simply seen on screen, there is also an overall decrease, for example, for BBC1 from 774 seconds in 1986 to 296 seconds in 1996. When the total number of appearances is taken into account, the average length of the seen appearance works out at 16 seconds in 1986 and 13 seconds in 1996. For *News at Ten* the respective average figures are 14 seconds and 11 seconds, with 24 and 14 seconds for *Channel Four News*.

Finally, how do British television news programmes cover the European Parliament or the European Union's Brussels location? In

Table 6.9: Political actors 'seen and heard' in primary items: total time in all locations by the number of appearances (Excluding House of Lords)

| | 1986 | | | 1996 | | | |
	Total time in secs	Total appearances	1 ÷ 2 = average in secs	Total time in secs	Total appearances	1 ÷ 2 = average in secs	Average change 1986 to 1996
BBC I	681*	35	19.5	636	48	13.3	(-) 6.2
ITN	616	36	17.1	483*	37	13.1	(-) 4
Channel 4	3,025	52	58.2	1,750	64	27.3	(-) 30.9

*9 days of news bulletins only.

general, the coverage of European issues tends to be refracted through British concerns and perspectives and, consequently, there are few instances when European issues – even with a British inflection – obtain any coverage which is unique to them. In fact, there were few occasions in our sample when European Union locations featured strongly: in 1996, the three main channels carried eight such items across the two-week sample (Channel 4 and ITN carried three each, BBC1 carried only two). There were some other items with a European theme but which had no European location, but here again the total number of items was small: three for the BBC, two for Channel 4 and two for ITN. However, this was during a period when the beef crisis was quite prominent. In 1986 *Channel Four News* carried three items, *News at Ten* carried three, and the *Nine O'Clock News* carried four.

Apart from the slight difference in the total number of such items – eight in 1996, ten in 1986 – one significant difference between the two years is that in 1986 there were at least some sound and pictures from locations in the European Community (as it was then), including the European Parliament.

In both years, prominent issues were the subject of most of the items. Five of the eight items in 1996 concerned the beef crisis, and five of the ten items in 1986 were about South Africa. The other items were about a variety of subjects such as defence, sport and finance in 1996, and the Middle East in 1986. The overall analysis of this part of the larger sample data shows that in 1996, only 193 seconds of European locations were used of which 78 seconds included domestic British politicians (principally Home Secretary Michael Howard), compared with 806 seconds in 1986 of which 427 seconds showed British domestic political actors (principally Foreign Secretary Geoffrey Howe). In neither case can this be said to be extensive coverage.

Sky News

In order to provide a comparison with the main terrestrial channels' news programmes, the 6.00 pm news programme on Sky was chosen for detailed analysis. In all cases, the same weeks were selected. However, the analysis of *Sky News* differs in many respects from the analysis of the other programmes examined above. Unlike the other three national news programmes, *Sky News* has been in operation only from the late 1980s and it is thus comparatively young. More significantly, though, it is a rolling news programme which is updated on the hour. Consequently, different bulletins may differ from one another as stories are revised, dropped or remain unchanged.

Another difference between Sky and the terrestrial news programmes is format. In 1996 Sky had two newsreaders, whose style was less formal than that of their competitors. The format is also more flexible than that of other programmes. On one day, for instance, an item on football violence which featured Michael Howard (Home Secretary) was followed by the newsreaders interviewing an author of a book on football violence. Similarly, film reviews can be woven into the programme on appropriate days. Finally, the sports section of the programme can be quite long. One bulletin contained a sports section of over four minutes (out of a 27-minute programme, inclusive of weather news). All this makes for a more popular and possibly populist news programme. Given this background, it is not surprising to find the political and parliamentary content to be quite different in kind. Some comparisons with the terrestrial services will be offered later on to emphasize this point.

However, it is not possible to make comparisons with the content of *Sky News* bulletins from the mid-1980s in the way that has been done with the other news programmes. It was decided instead to compare the 1996 output of *Sky News* with output from 1989 (prior to the introduction of television cameras into the House of Commons). Other problems then became apparent. *Sky News* has no archive of news programmes for 1989 but it does retain a copy of all the items broadcast from that year. Unfortunately, the cataloguing of these items was still in its infancy then and so there was no totally accurate record of what items were made and broadcast and of the times at which they might have been broadcast. Moreover, these items contained only the reporting packages inserted into the news programmes; there were no introductions or links between such packages. It is not possible, therefore, to make an assessment of the place of the selected packages within the overall news programme.

To overcome some of these pitfalls, a list of all the items which were classified as political – because they contained political actors, mentions of parliament, politics and the like – during the sample period was used as a framework from which to select appropriate items for analysis. From that list, all the items transmitted at 6.00 pm and 7.00 pm were then picked out for detailed analysis. Using this system ensured a high degree of probability that most, if not all, the political items broadcast during the main evening news programmes would be analysed. The obvious problem, though, is that the sample would be much larger than the 1996 sample since it was based on two, rather than one, evening news transmissions.

The 1996 news programmes

Excluding the links between items, and counting the sports news sections as one item (even though there may be information about different sports or events), the analysis identified 98 individual items in the nine bulletins analysed. (One day's programme was accidentally missed.) One bulletin had 14 items, two had nine, with the others having ten or eleven. These figures are not very different from those one can find for either BBC1's or ITN's news programmes, although the *Sky News* programme is a little shorter in length, running to about 24 minutes, excluding the advertisements and the weather reports. Of these 98 items, 18 were coded as primary political and a further 12 as items in which no more than a reference was made to a political actor. These latter 12 items will not form part of the detailed analysis presented below. There were no secondary political items.

The longest primary political item identified in the sample was 154 seconds (2 minutes 34 seconds); the shortest was 23 seconds. Of the 18 primary political items identified, seven were over 2 minutes (just) and 11 were under 2 minutes. The average length of the 18 items was 108 seconds, compared with ITN's 135 seconds and BBC1's 155 seconds.

Although the subjects of the items coded differed little from the subjects coded for the other channels – they included, for example, items on the beef crisis, Ireland, the Scott Inquiry into the sale of arms to Iraq – the placing of these items in the running order of the bulletin was quite different. On only three of the nine days did a primary political story lead the news bulletin. On one day, one such item was second in the running order and on five days a political story was third in the running order. In other words, nine items took up three positions out of a possible total of 27. The comparable figure for BBC1 (over ten bulletins) is 14 out of 30; for ITN, 10 out of 27; and for Channel 4, 18 out of 30 (Table 6.3).

As with the other research, it is possible to identify all the political actors featured in the news programmes. Twenty-two named politicians made a total of 45 separate appearances, with John Major (prime minister) making 11 appearances and Tony Blair (leader of the opposition) five. Three other politicians appeared more than once each (Howard, the home secretary, twice; Prescott, the deputy leader of the opposition, and Peter Thurnham, resigning Conservative MP, three times each), with a long list of others bringing up the total to 45. All these political actors were seen and 'seen and heard' for a total of 635 seconds, compared with a total of 932 seconds on BBC1 (ten bulletins) and for 769 seconds on ITN (nine bulletins). The three political party leaders took up 39% of all the time in which these political actors were seen and 'seen and heard' but only 32% of time taken by all actors seen speaking. As with the earlier data, neither Tony Blair nor Paddy Ashdown was seen and heard from outside the chamber (see Table A15).

The locations of all these appearances are many and various. The House of Commons at Question Time features prominently (in 21 of the 45 appearances) with other locations such as conferences, offices, courts also featuring but obviously less prominently. In the sample periods the exterior of the Palace of Westminster also featured on at least three occasions, as did Downing Street with the typical images of ministers arriving or leaving. There were 15 appearances in non-political locations such as in offices, in parks or outside unidentifiable buildings. Overall, though, *Sky News* gives less time to political actors, with the prime minister occupying one-third of all time devoted to political actors seen and heard in the chamber: 69 seconds out of a total of 204.

The 1989 news programme
The difficulty of making straight comparisons with an earlier year – in this case 1989 – have already been mentioned. The material offered below should thus be seen as a rough guide to some of the differences which can be identified between the two sample periods. The sampling procedure, imperfect as it was, produced a list of 28 items featuring political actors, and a further six items which only made reference to political actors, which

were (probably) transmitted at either 6.00 pm or 7.00 pm during the chosen sample weeks. This compares with only 18 items chosen for detailed analysis in 1996, though these were drawn from one news bulletin (6.00 pm) while the 28 items listed above were drawn from two bulletins.

The analysis of each of these items does, however, yield some interesting information – though not perhaps with respect to the range of subject matter. As with the other news programmes, the bulletins are heavily news-driven and in 1989 the major story was that of the tragedy at Hillsborough where nearly 100 football supporters were crushed to death. This tragedy featured in nine (33%) of the total items sampled. Other newsworthy subjects made up the running order, for instance the internal politics of the Labour Party, regulation of public houses, water privatization and so on.

Perhaps the most interesting point of comparison is that of the featured location of appearances made by political actors. As Table 6.10 shows, the sorts of locations identifiable in the news programmes have changed quite considerably, with a greater focus on the Chamber of the House. This, it should be recalled, is a pattern similar to the one experienced in the other news programmes.

Figure 6.8 compares the locations used for John Major in 1996 and Margaret Thatcher in 1989, although it is important to stress that the way the samples were drawn does not make them directly comparable.

With regard to the total time political actors were seen and 'seen and heard' in these items, comparisons with the 1996 sample are of little value. The figures are presented for the sake of completeness but they

Table 6.10: Number of times political actors appear in different locations, 1989 and 1996

Location	1989, n = 46	1996, n = 45
Chamber of the Commons	1	21
In a studio	7	3
Downing Street	5	2
Environs of Westminster	7	3
European location	4	1
Other location (inc. not known)	20	15
House of Lords	1	–
As photo	1*	–

*A photo was also used to supplement an appearance elsewhere.

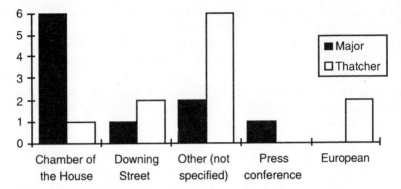

*Major (10 appearances) and Thatcher (11 appearances). Samples not directly comparable – see discussion in text.

Figure 6.8: Locations of main appearance of two prime ministers*

should be treated with great care since they are drawn from different samples and contain some features of coverage which were in evidence in 1986 but not in 1996. There were, for example, five interviews with key political actors in a studio. These items contributed 383 seconds to a total of 789 seconds in which political actors were seen and heard; the figure for 1996 is 372 seconds (see Table A16).

Overall, then, the difficulty of making year-on-year comparisons cannot be underestimated, although the comparisons made above do indicate a shift towards greater use of images and sound from the House. Whether this is to the detriment of other locations is an interesting question, since it presents the reverse of the argument which has been put up against the press and its political coverage in the 1990s.

Regional news

Also included in the research were regional news programmes, which provide a full continuum from the very formal and politically well-informed *Channel Four News* to the regional and more parochial sort of news bulletin. Given the nature of regional news programmes, and the low number of appearances by national political actors, it is probably not very useful to examine these news bulletins in as much detail as was required for the others. Generally speaking, regional news programmes do not make great use of national political actors, calling upon them in certain circumstances and when local stories warrant it. One item, for example, on pollution from power stations ended with a statement from Dennis Skinner, the local Labour MP. Comparisons with 1986 only reinforce these conclusions: national political actors make appearances when there is a connection with a local story or event, be it a by-election or a bid to host the Olympics.

This pattern suggests that the main national news programmes portray the institutional face of politics with national political actors playing a dominant part in the topics covered. Other news programme give a very minor role to such actors and use them sparingly. Furthermore, there is a different quality to the appearances of political actors on regional programmes. Whereas in national programmes they are protagonists, in regional ones they are much less so. In the national news programmes, national political actors are clearly identified with their institutional workplace or workplaces, in the regional news programmes with their more domestic settings and much less as key actors. They are not totally absent from regional news programmes but they merely play a different role.

Summary

A more detailed consideration of the significance of these comparisons will be reserved for the concluding chapter. Here we will only seek to draw out some of the more important findings as a way of recalling the initial widespread concern expressed about the coverage of parliament and politics, namely that there has been a decline in the coverage of parliament. As earlier chapters have confirmed, this has been the case for two out of the three newspapers analysed here, and quite dramatically so. Change in both these cases has been quite dramatic. Change in television news programmes on the main terrestrial channels has, however, been less marked. In many areas of coverage there has been a change, nonetheless. In 1996 compared to 1986:

- there were fewer primary political items;
- political actors were seen in fewer different locations;
- political actors, especially the party leaders, were seen and heard mainly in the House;
- the number of political actors seen, and the number of appearances made, had declined;
- the average length of a political actor's sound-bite had decreased.

In many of these cases, the changes have not been very large. Consequently, and as has been argued, television is not the medium of concern – at the moment. Proposed changes to news programmes or the advent of more popular news formats – along the lines of *Sky News* or *News on Five* – may change all this as the terrestrial channels adapt to the new news environment. What does emerge from these findings, though, is just how little use is made of the newly gained access to sound and images from the House.

Chapter 7

German and French newspaper coverage of parliament

The British data highlighted a change in newspaper coverage of parliament and political institutions between 1986 and 1996. Some of those changes were due, it has been argued, to the changing pressures which newspapers in Britain have been placed under in the past decade. Others, it was suggested, were the outcome of a change in the perceived importance of parliament. As was seen in Chapter 1, such a perception of change reflects a longer-term concern about how parliaments can adapt in an age where the media often do dictate the pattern, and the requirements, of political coverage.

Were these sorts of changes in evidence in other countries? To answer these questions, and in particular questions relating to changes in coverage, an attempt was made to replicate the British study in France and in Germany. The collected data do throw some light on the changes which have taken place in respect of parliamentary and political coverage in these two other countries, although on a limited number of occasions slightly different interpretations of the data make direct comparisons in certain areas problematic. For instance, the primary and secondary distinction in the German data is not directly comparable to the distinction made in the British data. More critically, it proved impossible to collect and analyse French newspaper data from 1986 so that particular point of comparison is not available. The following two sections review the analysis of German and French newspapers.

German press coverage of parliament and politics: overview of the data

The two German newspapers analysed, the *Süddeutsche Zeitung* (*SDZ*) and the *Frankfurter Allgemeine Zeitung* (*FAZ*), are both prominent dailies. *FAZ* has been described as Germany's leading quality paper; it has a circulation of around 400,000 and a political hue very similar to that of the conservative *Daily Telegraph*. *SDZ* is a quality regional newspaper with a substantial national readership and its politics is regarded as Left liberal. It had a circulation of over 300,000 in 1993. Both papers are considered to be examples of supranational newspapers, with a small circulation but a great deal of political influence (see Humphreys, 1996: 80–82).

Unlike the British – and to an extent the French – press, the German press has to report on a German parliament (the Bundestag) which meets less often than the parliaments in the two other countries in this study. Whereas the 15-day sample of British and French newspapers in both 1986 and 1996 was based around a period in which the respective parliaments would be meeting continuously, the identical 15 days did not always coincide with the sessions of the Bundestag. Consequently, the German newspaper sample for both years is made up of a larger number of days when the Bundestag was not in session than when it was. The distinction is not noted in the analysis presented here, which is based on all the data.

As with the data drawn from the British press, the main subject areas covered are fairly well represented in the sampled years (Table A17) although there were changes in the number of items carried by both these newspapers: the *Süddeutsche Zeitung* carried fewer political items in 1996 than in 1986, the *Frankfurter Allgemeine Zeitung* more. There are some differences, though. Changes in the political landscape of Germany have meant that the former East German states feature more prominently as subjects for inclusion in 1996 than in 1986, and the old states feature correspondingly less prominently. Such changes in news agendas are not unexpected and have affected other areas. The focus on European issues has also shifted: concerns about Europe in a domestic setting appear to be on the increase, while those about European issues outside Germany seem to be on the decrease. In the same vein, economic policy issues – perhaps themselves related to the new states – show a dramatic increase (from 5% to 19% for the *SDZ*, and from 7% to 16% for the *FAZ*). Figure 7.1 sets out the data for the German and British newspapers.

The drop in the number of items for the *SDZ*, for example, is small (12%) compared with that of the *Guardian* (27%) and the *Telegraph*

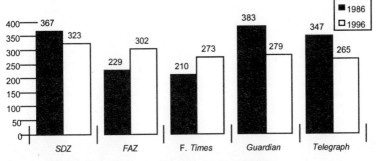

*Includes primary and secondary political items for the British press.

Figure 7.1: All items coded for German and British newspapers, 1986 and 1996*

(25%), though the increase in the number of items for the *FAZ* is only a little larger (32%) than the change experienced by the *Financial Times* (30%).

The two German newspapers have two common features. First, there has been a decrease in the number of political items which appeared on the front pages of both these newspapers. In the case of the *Frankfurter Allgemeine Zeitung*, the numerical decrease (two items) is compounded by the increase in the total number of items coded (Table 7.1).

Table 7.1: Items on the front page, *SDZ* and *FAZ*

SDZ 1986, n = 367	SDZ 1996, n = 323	FAZ 1986, n = 229	FAZ 1996, n = 302
13 %	10 %	21%	15 %
47 items	31 items	48 items	46 items

Second, with respect to the distribution of space as between photographs, headlines and text, there is one similarity with the British press: the German papers now devote more space to photographs – *SDZ* two-and-a-half times as much as it did in 1986, *FAZ* over ten times. As regards the space taken up by text, the two German newspapers have moved in opposite directions – not unlike some of the differences between the *Guardian* and the *Telegraph*, and the *Financial Times*. While the *SDZ* devoted less space to text in 1996 than in 1986, the *FAZ* gave substantially more space (Table 7.2).

Table 7.2: Percentage of item space taken up by photos, text and headlines, *SDZ* and *FAZ*

	Photos	Headline	Text	Total size of all items	Percentage change +/-
SDZ 1986 n = 367	2	14	84	51,767 cm. sq.	
SDZ 1996 n = 323	4	16	80	46,375 cm. sq.	–10
FAZ 1986 n = 229	1	11	88	34,004 cm. sq.	
FAZ 1996 n = 302	6	10	84	59,054 cm. sq.	+74

Locations of items

What are the locations of the coded items? Figure 7.2 (and Table A18) shows that there are fewer items located outside parliament, and more located in departments and in the European Commission. One important difference between the newspapers, though, is that the *SDZ* has fewer items located in parliament in 1996 than in 1986 (38 items as against 53, a drop from 15% to 12% of all items coded). In overall percentage terms, the total number of items located 'in parliament' has not changed much across the two years for the *FAZ* (16.2% to 17.5%) although the actual increase in the number of items has been more marked: 37 items in 1986 to 53 in 1996.

Other data confirm the general pattern identified above. The number of items over 50% of which took place in the Bundestag went up for the *Frankfurter Allgemeine Zeitung* from 26 in 1986 (11%) to 65 items in 1996 (22%). For the *Süddeutsche Zeitung* the figures are more complicated given that the total number of items coded decreased. Nevertheless, it carried 51 such items in 1986 (14%) and 50 in 1996 (15%).

Though the figures are broadly similar across many of the locations listed – including, for example, the 'in parliament' category which is a composite of many activities in the Bundestag, including committees – the slight variations in the actual number of items coded which did occur alter some of the more obvious interpretations. For instance, for the *FAZ*

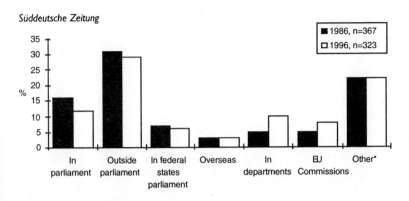

Süddeutsche Zeitung

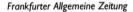

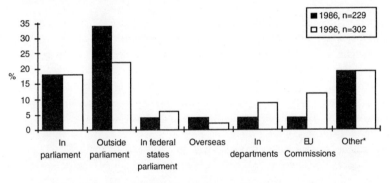

Frankfurter Allgemeine Zeitung

*Includes cases where data indeterminate or not applicable.
Note: Figures relate to 97% of all items for *SDZ*, and 96% for *FAZ*.

Figure 7.2: Percentage of items in different locations, *SDZ* and *FAZ*

the 'in parliament' category is similar across both years, yet in 1986, 2% (or five items) were about committees. There were no such items in 1996. More importantly, though the outside parliament category shows a large drop, from 34% to 22%, the actual numbers involved are not so very different: 77 items in 1986 but only 67 in 1996. In other words, the increase in the total number of items coded for the *FAZ* makes a small decrease appear larger in percentage terms.

The German data are thus unlike the British: one does not find the same sharp drop in interest in politics and parliament as one did for two

Table 7.3: A comparison of German and British items in sample

	SDZ 1986, n=367	SDZ 1996, n=323	FAZ 1986, n=229	FAZ 1996, n=302	Gdn 1986, n=383	Gdn 1996, n=279	Teleg 1986, n=347	Teleg 1996, n=265
Parliamentary in parliament	25% 91 items	21% 68 items	22% 50 items	29% 88 items	26% 100 items	16% 45 items	27% 92 items	16% 42 items
Parliamentary out of parliament	41% 149 items	37% 118 items	40% 91 items	25% 76 items	39% 151 items	35% 97 items	28% 98 items	33% 86 items

of the three British papers analysed earlier (Figure 7.1) or in terms of items which are mostly located in the parliament. This latter point provides a good contrast between the different sets of newspapers. As with the British data, all the items were coded in such a way as to determine, wherever possible, whether the events or matters described in the item took place within the parliamentary institution (parliamentary in parliament) or outside (parliamentary out of parliament). The German data are more complex than the British since some of the items were coded as 'parliamentary in parliament' in respect of the regional as opposed to federal parliament. Overall, about one-fifth of all items coded as 'parliamentary in parliament' dealt with the regional parliaments. Even taking this into consideration, one finds that the pattern of change falls into line with the data above (Table 7.3). This comparison identifies the divergence between the two sets of national papers, with the British ones moving away more sharply from parliament as a focus of news coverage.

Coverage of political actors

As with the British data, it is possible to assess the ways in which German political actors are represented in German newspapers. This can be done in two ways. First, one can look at groupings of actors: groupings such as ministers, opposition, and so on. Second, one can look at individually named political actors. With regard to the various groupings identifiable from the data, it is surprising that the *Bundeskanzler*, the Chancellor, does not play a more prominent role. For the two newspapers, and for the two years Helmut Kohl was mentioned as the first actor in a political item eight times or less. Others, such as the economics ministers Rexrodt or Bangemann, sometimes appear or appeared more often (Tables A19–21). There were even fewer mentions as a second and third actor. Once more, a comparison with the British data suggests that the British prime minister appears more prominently in news items – at least into double figures and more consistently across first, second and third position in any political item coded (see Tables A8 and A9). What the figures also show is that the pattern of change in the newspapers analysed is related to the decrease or increase in the total number of items coded: as the *SDZ* has fewer items in 1996 than in 1986, so fewer individual political actors occupy first position. The opposite is true for the *FAZ*.

That said, government ministers, the government, the opposition and *Land* political actors play a significant part in news coverage and are prominent. Not surprisingly, ministers are mentioned very often – 21% of all first references to political actors in 1986 for the *SDZ*, and 18% in 1996; for the *FAZ* the respective figures are 23% and 21% – with the other groupings trailing behind. When combined, it is clear that the ruling bloc obtains most references: as before, governments act and others react, partially explaining the pattern of coverage (Table A19).

Finally, are there fewer political actors making an appearance in these items between one year and another and one paper and another? The important point which emerges most clearly is that the total number of actors quoted directly, indirectly or both falls, or rises, in line with the number of items coded for the newspapers. So, as the number of *SDZ* items declines, so too does the number of actors quoted (from 280 to 183) but the reverse is the case for the *FAZ* (increase from 116 to 163). Again, this is in contrast with the British data where, as we have seen, the number of actors – certainly in parliamentary page items – declines. Individual political actors within this broader picture are not very heavily represented and few are mentioned in the leading actors' position more than five times on either paper or in either year (Table A22).

Political coverage in the French press

The study of the French press is incomplete by comparison with the study of either the British or the German press in that data for 1986 are unavailable. Consequently, whilst it may be possible to make comparisons across countries, it is not possible to make comparisons over time. Nevertheless, in many other respects, the French study broadly replicates the British and German ones and similar questions can be asked across all three contexts.

Three newspapers featured in the French press and these were chosen to reflect the available range of elite newspapers: *Le Figaro*, *Le Monde* and *Libération*. *Le Figaro* is owned by Robert Hersant and is generally considered a Gaullist paper. *Le Monde* is often seen to provide an independent political voice on matters of state though it has had its political favourites on the Left (Mitterrand, for example). *Libération*, by contrast, has often been described as a leading and radical European newspaper and had in the past competed directly with *Le Monde* to be the active voice of the Left. In terms of circulation, these three Paris-based dailies are regarded as reaching the decision-makers: in the early 1990s *Libération's* circulation was around 183,000, *Le Monde's* 380,000 and *Le Figaro's* 420,000. More significantly, two of the three papers are of fairly recent origin: *Libération* was first published as a 'leftist' paper in 1973, while *Le Monde* came into existence in 1944 (Thibau, 1996).

Of the three newspapers, *Le Figaro* and *Le Monde* provide the more comprehensive coverage of politics generally, if one takes the number of coded items as an indicator: 196 items were coded for *Le Figaro*, 190 for *Le Monde* but only 128 for *Libération*. This is not surprising given their different approaches: *Le Monde* has traditionally carried few photographs and its presentation can best be described as sober, and this emerges quite clearly in the data. Whereas 62% of the total space devoted to the coded items in *Le Figaro* comprised text, the corresponding figure for *Le Monde* is 87%. *Le Figaro* also gave more space to headlines than did *Le Monde* (Table 7.4).

Table 7.4: Percentage of space taken up by coded items, three French newspapers, 1996

	Text	Headline	Photo
Le Figaro	61	25	14
Le Monde	87	10	3
Libération	63	13	24

The three newspapers analysed also show some differences of emphasis or agenda (or both) with regard to the subjects of items coded. For example, *Le Monde* carried more items about European issues but fewer general political items than the other two newspapers, but in other respects there are some strong similarities between them (Table A23).

Table 7.5: Primary location of item, three French newspapers (%)

	Assemblée Nationale	Commissions	Senate	Other political institution*	European Union/ Parliament	Outside institutions and other location	Ministries
Le Figaro	19	1	3	4	16	52	5
Le Monde	8	3	4	4	13	68	–
Libération	13	1	3	6	11	62	4

*This includes the President, speakers or councils of ministers.

What of the focus on the parliamentary institution? As Table 7.5 shows, both the National Assembly and the European Parliament and Commission are important locations, the latter particularly so since it is by no means so important for either the British or German press. Nevertheless, nearly half of the coded political items are located outside the political settings listed.

The main focus of the coded items and the emphasis placed on the main institutional political actors can be seen in the next two figures. Figure 7.3 sets out the percentage of items which are focused on key categories of political actors, while Figure 7.4 looks at the number of items which take place in five main locations, including the Matignon, the prime minister's official residence.

The strong institutional focus is evident in both these figures.

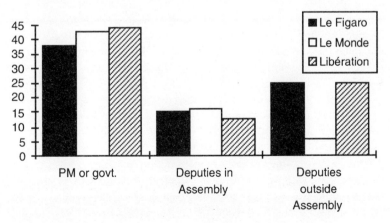

Figure 7.3: Focus of items in three French newspapers (%)

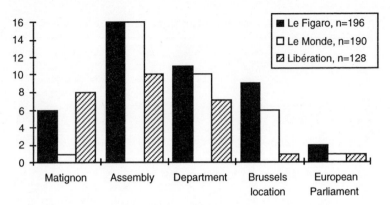

**Figure 7.4: Percentage of items with over 50% of item in five
political locations, three French newspapers**

Political actors in the coded items

Political actors feature quite strongly in the coded political items and, as
in the German sample but unlike in the British sample, the number of
political and other actors mentioned declines quite rapidly: for example,
nearly 50% of *Le Figaro*'s items have no fifth actor (or more) mentioned.
This means that the number of actors mentioned is concentrated into the
first few possible placings; as one goes into the individual items, the
occurrence of identified actors declines rapidly. For these reasons, only
the first three positions or placings will be explored here.

In the 1996 data, the most important single political actor is
undoubtedly Alain Juppé, the prime minister. In the *Le Figaro* sample, he
featured in first position in 12% of all the coded items (or 23 times)
though this declined quite rapidly to 5% of items in second position, and
3% of items in third position. In *Le Monde*, the same pattern is in
evidence: first placing in 10% of all the items (or 18 items), second
position in 8% of all items, third position in 4% of all items. When certain
categories of actors are combined, for example Juppé and his advisers, or
the Left, the importance of the prime minister remains although the combined importance of other groupings increases. The president (Jacques
Chirac in 1996) is much less prominent (Table A24).

In keeping with the data from the other two countries, those in power
are given greater access to the press than others (Table A24), and this
applies also to who is mentioned most often. Across all three newspapers,
for instance, it is Chirac and Juppé who are most often mentioned in the

Table 7.6: Percentage of items consisting of quotes, three French newspapers

	No quotes	Under 50%	Over 50%
Le Figaro	25	65	13
Le Monde	28	69	3
Libération	10	84	7

political items coded. Perhaps more interesting – at least in the context of discussions about the extent to which parliamentary institutions are reported extensively and directly – few of the political items consisted of substantial quotes (Table 7.6) and, therefore, large amounts of verbatim coverage of debates or speeches.

Given the limited nature of the analysis of French newspapers, it is difficult to draw any generalizations beyond the ones mentioned here. The final chapter will review some of these findings in the context of a comparison with data from both Germany and Britain.

Chapter 8

German and French television coverage of parliament

For both the German and French broadcast media, two weeks of television news programmes from 1986 and 1996 bulletins were recorded and coded. (Full details are in Appendix 1.) For both media, an attempt was made to replicate the main lines of research developed and undertaken in respect of the British media. One important difference, though, is that the analysis of the British media used two categories for television news items – primary and secondary – which were unfortunately conflated in the analysis of the broadcast media of the two other countries. The significance, or otherwise, of this will become clearer as the findings are reported. All items which fell into our broad definition of a political item were identified for the purpose of further analysis. In the case of the broadcast media, the length of an item was taken to include the main report on a subject by, say, a journalist *and* the newsreader's or link person's introduction to it. This practice was adopted across all broadcast media.

German television news

The news programmes chosen are of a different length and they are each transmitted at a different time. Arbeitsgemeinschaft der Rundfunkanstalten Deutschlands (ARD's) programme, *Taggeschau*, is transmitted at 8.00 pm and runs for 15 minutes, while Zweites Deutsches Fernsehen's (ZDF's) *Heute* runs for about 20 minutes from 7.00 pm. In 1986, *Heute* was longer and ran for some 30 minutes. These two news programmes, and the two television services, are part of Germany's public broadcasting system and may therefore be quite different from the commercial services such as SAT1 and RTL Plus which have since come to play such a big part in German broadcasting. Moreover, the two services selected have their own characteristic features. These were described by Barbara Pfetsch as follows:

> The content of public channels was characterized at the time [1986] by a comparatively high amount of political information and by a portrayal of politics in which the orientation towards the political elite was a more important concern than the presentational format of the programme. (1996: 435)

Pfetsch goes on to argue that there has since been a change in the presentational nature of the public broadcasters' news programmes although the content of the news programmes themselves has remained much the same. Some of the data from her own work suggest change but not necessarily drastic change, as we shall see. More generally, her data offer some possibility of comparison between different studies though there are differences between this study and her own which make detailed comparisons difficult.

As far as this study is concerned, there is evidence of a decrease in the number of items coded as 'political' within the terms of this study – that is, items which are primarily political and which have a political actor taking part in a significant capacity. However, as there were very few secondary political items, these were included in the main body of the analysis. Conversely, the items analysed did not include those which were essentially foreign political stories but which may have featured a domestic political actor in a very minor capacity. In any case, there were only 26 such items across both years and programmes. By excluding this category, the items coded and analysed were thus principally domestic political items.

The overview of the data shows a reduction in the number of political items coded, particularly for ZDF – which may be due in part to the reduction in the length of the programme (Table 8.1).

Table 8.1: Total items and total domestic political items, German TV

	Total items, 1986	Domestic political items*	Total items, 1996	Domestic political items*
ZDF	201	67	158 (−21%)	36 (−46%)
ARD	157	63	164 (+4%)	54 (−14%)

*These are all primary and secondary items of a domestic nature.

Do these figures correspond with those of Barbara Pfetsch (1996)? Direct comparisons are difficult partly because her sample is of four weeks drawn from 1985/6 and four weeks drawn from 1993. Moreover, her own comparisons are between public channels and private channels so it is not possible to separate ARD from ZDF. Nonetheless, it is interesting to note that Pfetsch coded a total of 2,172 items from ARD's 1985/6 news output over a four-week period and 2,077 from ZDF's news output. These figures are far in excess of the ones coded for this project for 1986 (see Table 8.1), but they include *all* regular news broadcasts and evening news magazines and they also come from four weeks of programme output (Pfetsch, 1996: 437). In 1993, and with only one news show coded for each of the public channels, Pfetsch's figures correspond more closely to the data here. For 1993, she coded 498 items from ARD's *Taggeschau, Taggesthemen* and 563 from ZDF's *Heute, Heute Journal*. These figures are just over twice the number coded for this study and could be explained by the double size of the Pfetsch sample. Generally, then, one can argue that the number of items coded in 1993 by Pfetsch are broadly similar, thus permitting some very limited comparisons.

The drop in the number of items recorded in Table 8.1 has had an obvious impact on the overall length of time devoted to such items but it has not had a major impact on the average length of each item broadcast. These still hover around the 95–100 second mark (Table 8.2). In that sense, then, the change across the ten years has not been very significant – though the average length has gone up rather than down. Looking at the distribution of these items across broad categories of news, one becomes aware of some differences between the two German television services (for example, there are fewer domestic items for the ARD service than for ZDF), but the overall pattern shows a fairly constant mix of categories (Figure 8.1).

Table 8.2: Total and average length of domestic political items, German TV

	Political items	Total time, secs	Average
ARD, 1986	63	5473	87
ARD, 1996	54	5177 (−5%)	96
ZDF, 1986	67	6342	95
ZDF, 1996	36	4196 (−34%)	117

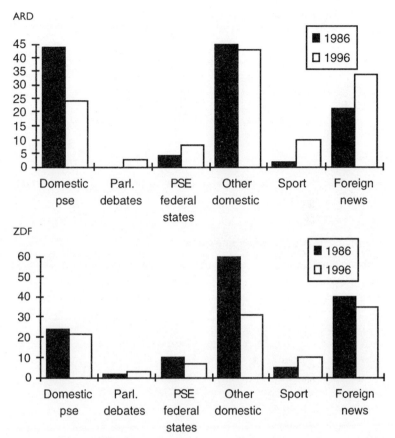

Figure 8.1: Distribution of items into major categories, German TV

What of the prominence of the coded items? As with the British analysis, by looking at the location of each item in the overall running order it is possible to assess how prominent they were in any one programme. Figure 8.2 outlines the findings and places the items in the main running order following the news headlines and trailers at the start of all programmes.

Once again, although there are fewer items in 1996, the prominence of the coded items has, in some cases, actually increased. For example, whereas 47% of ZDF's coded items in 1986 featured in the first six items of the bulletins, in 1996 the figure had increased to 64%. This is in contrast with the findings from the British study (see Table 6.3).

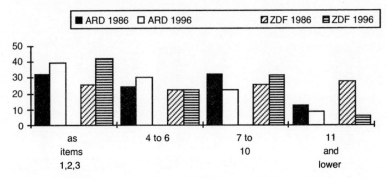

Figure 8.2: Percentage of items in different positions in the running order, German TV

Political actors in German news items

Although up to 15 actors could be coded for each item, no item included very many actors and most items included actors only to about the tenth position. Had their importance changed over the ten-year period and, if so, in what way?

Table 8.3 shows how much time of the coded political items was given over to these political actors. These data are based on the sorts of calculations carried out for the British part of the research and distinctions are made here, as elsewhere, between those instances when political actors are merely seen and when they are 'seen and heard' – that is, when they are in view talking.

Table 8.3: Total political actors seen and 'seen and heard' in coded political items, German TV (seconds)

	1 *Seen*	*2* *Seen and* *heard*	*3* *Total col 1* *and 2*	*4* *Total item* *length*	*5* *Col 3 as %* *of col 4*
ARD 1986	858	1,000	1,858	5,473	**34**
ARD 1996	674	799	1,473	5,177	**28**
Change 1986 to 1996 (%)	**–21**	**–20**	**–21**	**–5**	
ZDF 1986	907	1,129	2,036	6,342	**32**
ZDF 1996	325	849	1,174	4,196	**28**
Change 1986 to 1996 (%)	**–64**	**–25**	**–42**	**–34**	

Overall, the total figures for 1996 are lower than for 1986 – actors are seen for less time, and are seen and heard for less time – particularly in the case of ZDF. However, when the decrease in the total length of items is taken into account (col 4 in Table 8.3) the percentage changes appear less dramatic (from 34% or 32% to 28%). Nevertheless, the crucial point to note is that the figures for 1996 are considerably lower than for 1986.

The more interesting question is whether the number of actors given access to the airwaves has changed. Figure 8.3 shows the total number of political actors seen on the two news programmes *in the first five positions only* in all coded political items; political actors appear in later positions but fairly infrequently.

Although the number of political actors seen on the screen has decreased in the case of ZDF, in line with the data in Table 8.3, there has not been a reduction for either service in the number of political actors 'seen and heard'. The same is broadly true of the number of appearances made by political actors (i.e. a political actor may make more than one appearance) but here the data point to a decrease in the time allocated to political actors: moreover each appearance in 1996 is shorter than in 1986. As with the British data, the length of time given to politicians to air comments has decreased quite substantially for both services (Table 8.4).

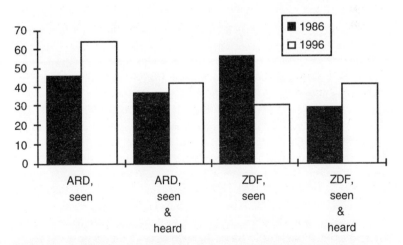

Figure 8.3: Number of political actors appearing in German TV news programmes, first five positions in domestic political items

Table 8.4: Length of appearances by political actors, German TV – all political items, all positions in which actors make an appearance*

Seen

	Total seen appearances, 1986	Total seen appearances, 1996	Average length of appearance, in secs, 1986	Average length of appearance, in secs, 1996	*Change 1986 to 1996, + / – in secs*
ARD	56	77	15	9	**–6**
ZDF	74	45	12	7	**–5**

Seen and heard

	Total seen appearances, 1986	Total seen appearances, 1996	Average length of appearance, in secs, 1986	Average length of appearance, in secs, 1996	*Change 1986 to 1996, + / – in secs*
ARD	41	58	24	14	**–10**
ZDF	37	55	31	15	**–16**

*These figures produce *total* figures which are a little different from those in Table 8.3 because of the practice of rounding up or down. The differences are in the region of 10 to 20 seconds overall out of totals of 800 seconds or so.

In both cases one can see a change in the time allocated to political actors when they make appearances in news bulletins.

Finally, which political actors are seen and 'seen and heard' most often and where? Certain political figures feature fairly often across the two channels and the two years of the sample but there is little sense of these political figures featuring so prominently as to dwarf all others. The Chancellor, Helmut Kohl, and a selection of ministers or contenders for high office appear most often both in 1986 and in 1996. In 1986, Kohl, Weizsäcker, President of the Federal Republic and Rau (candidate for chancellor) and Blum dominate, while in 1996, the four most prominent political actors were Kohl, Blum, Lafontaine and Kanther. Together, these actors account for some 30% of all appearances. More important, perhaps, is the change in the locations of these appearances. Figure 8.4 shows the more restricted range of locations in 1996 as compared with 1986.

If Figure 8.4 shows that the Bundestag in general is no longer used in 1996 as a backdrop for political actors to be seen against, the chamber

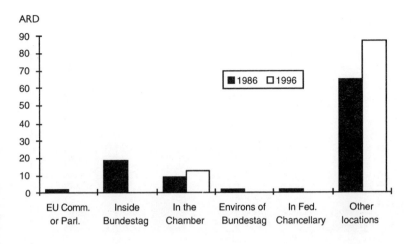

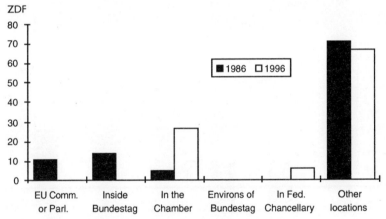

Figure 8.4: Location of seen appearances

itself has grown in prominence, as have other settings. The same pattern is visible when examining the settings in which political actors are seen and heard (Figure 8.5). The figures mask the raw data: the actual number of times actors were seen speaking in the chamber in 1996 was 11 for ARD and nine for ZDF; in 1986, the figures were six and eight respectively.

Finally, it is worth returning to Pfetsch's analysis for some comparative figures. Although her data show an increase in the percentage of news events referring to governmental action, they also indicate a *decrease* in the percentage of items referring to parliamentary debates

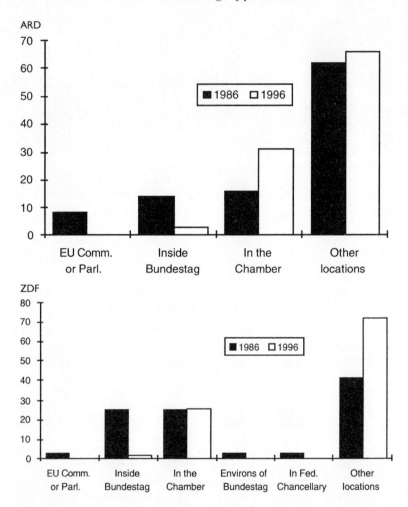

Figure 8.5: Actors seen and heard in different locations, German TV (%)

and to politicians' speeches across both ARD and ZDF (from 16.1% and 17.1% respectively in 1986 to 11.7% and 6.6% respectively in 1996) (1996: 442). In fact, in the eight years between 1985/6 and 1993, 'news events which had a clear reference to political institutions and actors decreased from 74% to 53%' for the public broadcasters (1996: 443). The pattern she reports is broadly in line with the findings from this study.

More direct comparisons between these data and the British (and French) data are provided in the final chapter.

Analysis of French television news programmes

The analysis of French television news was carried out with the same aims as the British and the German analysis. Here too, all items which contained political actors in an important role were analysed with a view to determining location, length of appearances and such like.

The two news programmes chosen were those of Antenne 2, later France 2 (A2/F2) and Télévision Française 1 (TF1). TF1 offers some insight into a service in the throes of privatization in the mid-1980s and fully privatized by the mid-1990s (see Kuhn, 1994). The impact of the changes in French broadcasting may be seen in some of the data below. The analysis presented here focuses on this comparison of output over the ten years. This analysis of the two services suggests some important differences across the two years with a major decline in the number of items coded in 1996: from 44 items for TF1 in 1986 to 25 items in 1996, and from 42 for A2/F2 in 1986 to 27 in 1996 (Table 8.5).

Table 8.5: French TV news coverage of political items, 1986 and 1996

	1986		*1996*	
	Total items	*Total time (secs)*	*Total items*	*Total time (secs)*
TF1	44	3,560	25	2,886
A2/F2	42	4,372	27	2,511

The drop in the total number of items is very marked and represents a decrease of between 35% and 45%. Whether this is simply due to particular circumstances in the weeks selected for this analysis is difficult to say. By chance, a third week of these two news programmes in 1996 was coded and the figures show up some differences across the sample period. In this third week, as Table 8.6 shows, 30 separate items were coded for TF1 and 26 for A2/F2. Because the two weeks – out of the three available – were chosen at random for further and detailed analysis, it is impossible to say which, if any, is the more typical week. However, there are other data available which can throw light on this matter, namely, two extra weeks analysed from 1989. Although the data from 1989, and their analysis, do not feature in this report, the number of items coded in those weeks are in line with the data used in the rest of this report. In other words, the number of items recorded in the third sample week for 1996 is out of step with the other available data.

Table 8.6: Number of items coded in each week of the years analysed, French TV*

	7–11 July '86	27–3 Oct '86	April '89	May '89	22–26 Jan '96	19–23 Feb '96	18–22 Mar '96
TFI	23	21	19	12	14	11	30
A2/F2	22	20	15	18	8	19	26

*The two weeks in 1986 and in 1996 analysed here are in bold.

The total time taken up by these items has generally declined – from 3,560 seconds to 2,886 seconds for TF1 and from 4,372 seconds to 2,511 seconds for A2/F2. Detailed analysis, however, shows that although the time taken up by political actors 'seen and heard' has declined, the total time political actors are seen only has actually increased. Of these two categories, it is the former which is obviously more important in a study such as this (Table 8.7).

The total number of actors seen increased for both channels, although the number of political actors 'seen and heard' remained the same for TF1 but decreased for A2/F2 from 20 to 14 actors. This pattern can also be found in the analysis of the number of appearances made by these political actors. All in all, then, the change for A2/F2 has been much more marked than it has been for TF1.

The table also shows that as with the British data the average length of the sound-bite – taken here to be the total seconds a political actor is seen and heard divided by the number of appearances – has declined: from 57 seconds in 1986 to 44 seconds in 1996 for TF1, and from 43 to 36 seconds for A2/F2. However, these are larger sound-bites than are available on either British or German television news.

As for who makes most appearances, the findings are not very surprising since they show that some key figures dominated the news programmes. In 1986, it was President Mitterrand who was the most prominent actor in the news programmes, followed by the prime minister,

Table 8.7: Time devoted to political actors/number of appearances made, French TV

	Seen 1986 in secs/no. of appearances	Average length of appearance in secs	Seen and heard 1986 in secs/no. of appearances	Average length of appearance in secs
TF1/F2	422 / 22	19	1,377 / 24	57
A2/F2	154 / 4	39 / 39	1,547 / 36	43

	Seen 1996 in secs/no. of appearances	Average length of appearance in secs	Seen and heard 1996 in secs/no. of appearances	Average length of appearance in secs
TF1	647 / 34	19	1,323 / 30	44
A2/F2	478 / 31	15	832 / 23	36

Jacques Chirac. That prominence was also translated into the duration of their appearances: Mitterrand was seen and heard for 384 seconds, 28% of all the 'seen and heard' time devoted to politicians on the screen in the case of TF1, and 311 seconds, or 20% in the case of A2/F2. Interestingly, only one of these 13 appearances was in a governmental location, namely, the Elysée or its environs. Jacques Chirac was on screen for much less time and took up only 12% of TF1's seen and heard category, and 10% of A2/F2's. Together, they occupied 40% of TF1 seen and heard time and 30% of A2/F2's.

The data for 1996 also emphasize the roles of the president (Chirac) and the prime minister (Juppé). Chirac is both seen and heard for 24% of all the 'seen and heard' time on TF1 and for 15% of the time allocated on A2/F2; Juppé's share is 6% and 5% respectively. Although these two political actors account for 37% of all appearances on TF1, and 35% of all appearances on A2/F2, there are other appearances by political actors that make substantial contributions to the total time in the 'seen and heard' category. For example, on TF1, Lionel Jospin's appearance occupied some 349 seconds – or about six minutes – which is much more than

115

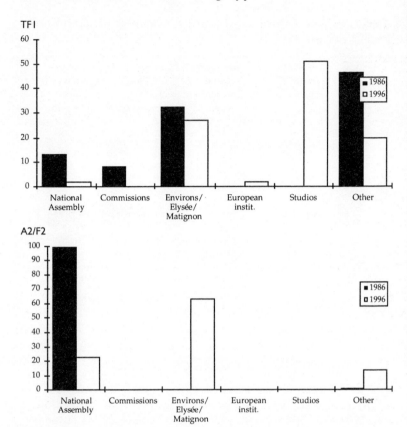

Figure 8.6: Locations in which political actors were seen, all items, French TV (%)

Chirac's 319 seconds. The same was true for A2/F2 where Laurent Fabius's sole appearance in the 'seen and heard' category was 242 seconds (four minutes), well in excess of Chirac's 127 seconds. So, some actors appear in short bursts more often than others who surface only occasionally.

Are there differences in the locations, as there were with the British and German data? In terms of where the political actors are simply *seen*, the data show a trend away from the Assemblée Nationale, with the other settings such as the Elysée, the Matignon, and studios becoming more in evidence. A different interpretation would be that the Assemblée Nationale was an important but not a significant location in either year

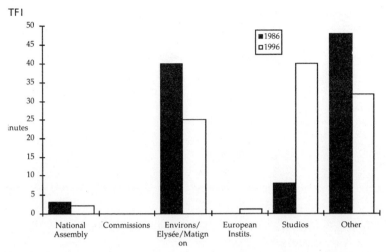

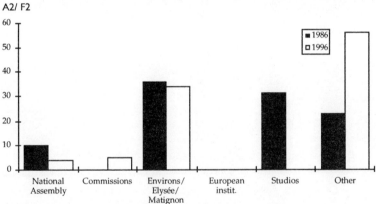

Figure 8.7: Locations in which political actors were 'seen and heard', all items, French TV (%)

analysed. Apart from in the 1986 data for A2/F2, it was not as significant a location as, say, the Elysée and Matignon. This second interpretation would also be true for the location of political actors when seen and heard. Only 10% or less of total time taken up by politicians in the 'seen and heard' category on either channel or in either year was accounted for by the National Assembly. Other locations such as the Elysée, Matignon and even studios were more important as locations (see Figures 8.6 and 8.7).

Table 8.8: Main subject focus of coded items, French TV

	TF1 1986		TF1 1996		A2/F2 1986		A2/F2 1996	
	no.	%	no.	%	no.	%	no.	%
Domestic pse	23	52	21	84	19	45	20	74
Parliamentary debates/activities	4	9	2	8	6	14	4	15
Other domestic	3	7	–		–		–	
France/EU relations	5	11	2	8	3	7	2	7
France and other countries	7	16	–		12	29	1	4
Foreign news	–		1	4	–		–	
Other	2	5	–		2	5	–	
Total	44		25		42		27	

Table 8.9: Number and percentage of coded items in French TV news programmes' running order

	TF1 1986		TF1 1996*		A2/F2 1986		A2/F2 1996	
	no.	%	no.	%	no.	%	no.	%
1–5	14	32	2	8	15	36	2	7
6–10	17	39	11	44	16	38	14	52
10–15	8	18	5	20	9	21	10	37
16 and lower	5	11	5	20	2	5	1	4

*Two items had information missing.

Although there is a decline in the prominence of the National Assembly as a location, it is a small decline from a low base. This suggests that the important venues for political communication are not the institutional ones of parliamentary chambers but others where questions and dialogues with reporters can take place. Furthermore, it supports the views expressed by correspondents that as a venue, the visual qualities of the National Assembly are clearly limited.

Most of the items coded dealt with domestic affairs, with a small number featuring parliamentary debates (Table 8.8). Overall, though, their placement in the running order had definitely changed in the two years analysed. In 1986, 32% and 36% of items were in locations 1 to 5 for TF1 and A2/F2 respectively but by 1996 only 8% and 7% were. In the next five positions, the respective figures were: 39% and 38% up to 44% for TF1 and 52% for A2/F2. There was an increase in items lower in the order, suggesting that political items were not as prominent in the running order of news programmes as they had been in 1986 (Table 8.9). This downgrading of the prominence of political items is in direct contrast to the findings from both Germany and, to a lesser extent, Britain. The next chapter returns to some other comparisons which can be drawn from the data.

Chapter 9

Summary and conclusions

The data presented in the above chapters chart the changes that have taken place in three countries and across different media. At times, the data allow for direct comparisons, at other times not. This chapter seeks to pull together many of the themes which have surfaced throughout and to connect these with the main aims and objectives of the research. The chapter is divided into three parts: the first part considers some of the comparisons as they relate to the press, the second looks at the data drawn from the analysis of television output, while the third offers a more general overview.

Before turning to the comparisons in detail, it is worth recalling what the research reported here sought to do. Briefly, the project was set up in such a way as to explore the changing nature of parliamentary and political coverage between 1986 and 1996 in three specific countries. The main point of reference was Britain – since it was here that the research was initiated and the research questions articulated and formulated – but certain connections were made with practices and data from both Germany and France. Comparisons between countries have proved more difficult than had at first been hoped, partly because of slightly different research and coding practices between the teams involved but perhaps more because of the very different political systems under investigation. The parliaments in question are not identical, the main traditions of journalism are different and the relationships between the worlds of politics and the media differ from one country to another. The research methodology adopted here, the pressures of time and the level of resources may not have created sufficient opportunities for such differences to be tackled in a more subtle and sophisticated way.

In the same vein, the points of convergence across media and across practices have not been fully analysed: they are part of a longer-term process which is much larger than the aims and objectives of this particular study. Yet there appear to be some interesting common points between the countries investigated. As we have seen, editors in Britain have abandoned the idea of parliament having any privileges over and above other institutions, while journalists have become bored with the visually unexciting nature of parliaments and have also had to rethink their approach to writing about parliament and politics for the modern multimedia audience. As our German parliamentary correspondent for a super-regional newspaper admitted:

> Processes in the Bundestag are complex and there are many different levels of decision-making. Because of this, you are confronted with the journalistic question of what you offer the public or what you expect of it. This task has been made more difficult for a range of broadcasters, particularly for the public stations, because of competition from private television companies. This is also noticeable because they frequently no longer report the process of a decision, only that one has been reached. *We are also discussing how far we should move in this direction.* Here ideas have changed to a certain extent. We should not offer a report or a tiny morsel every day but, at the appropriate time, we should summarize and, at the same time, explain the context. (Emphasis added)

Although this reporter denied that one could detect in Germany the sort of (extreme?) trend evidenced in some parts of the British press, he was fully aware of broader changes in the nature of journalism, of the need to rethink how to communicate and what to communicate, all within a changing media environment. Just as the public broadcasters have had to think about their work when faced by the private broadcasters, so the press has had to readjust its own work in relation to what the other media are doing. One extreme example of this would be the British newspaper journalists who saw television's political coverage as a reason not to undertake such coverage themselves (the availability of parliamentary proceedings on the Internet could be another reason); another example would be the French broadcast journalist who saw no reason to increase political coverage of parliament on the main channels on the grounds that dedicated channels would and could offer a better platform for this.

121

It is perhaps the search for a *more* appropriate or *the* most appropriate vehicle for political communication that lies at the heart of many of the points raised in this study. The direct reproduction of debates and similar oral content in newspapers has clearly fallen out of favour; a newer, more contextualized account is now available but this is an account of a much more restricted agenda. For its part, television is unwilling or unable to cope with the existing manner of parliamentary proceedings: speeches, deliberation, arguments are oddly unsuited to the needs and wants of either the 'MTV generation' or the 'three-minute culture'. Furthermore, these things cannot be the content of *popular* television services and it may be that they only have a future within more specialized venues specially carved out for them. The American model is CSPAN, the British is the Parliamentary Channel, the Internet will provide yet another model, and so on: all provide open access for specialized minorities. The danger in this sort of development is that the wider public may not feel the need to gain access to these services. With the older media systems, members of the public could not avoid such content as they skimmed the pages of their newspapers. In practice, as we have seen, not all newspapers carried such content or such content in large chunks.

Fundamentally, the problem remains: how can an institution which is seen as central to the conduct of democratic systems best be represented in the mass media? If discussion and debate are part of the process by which decisions are arrived at, should these not be represented also? Otherwise, why have parliaments, oppositions or debates? To claim, as journalists often do, that parliament and its work have changed ignores or overlooks the fact that journalists have also played a part in bringing about those changes. Different practices would most probably have brought about different changes, some of which might have been more advantageous to parliament; ignoring large parts of it, as the British broadsheets now do, may have had the opposite effect.

Nevertheless, the views of journalists on the changing role of parliamentary institutions cannot be ignored. As one surveys such institutions with their near empty chambers, one cannot help wondering whether parliaments have themselves worked out their duties and responsibilities in the modern global political age. How important – in mass media terms, in terms of the public interest, in political and economic terms – is a late-night sitting in which a score or so of MPs discuss a subject that is dear to their hearts? Clearly, not even they would expect *as of right* and *as a matter of routine* that the sitting be covered. However, this begs the question of what should be covered and why that and not something else.

It also begs the question of what form parliamentary coverage should take. Throughout these discussions, there has been an assumption that the desirable form is one that creates space for political actors, for their words and for their deeds. But is that form the most appropriate one? Is it not sometimes better to have political actors and their work interpreted within a broad political context or for their actions to be explained by journalists? This latter form is the one currently used by journalists and it does not preclude the use of extracts from statements of debates. It is, in other words, a different way of covering the world of the political actor and it might have become accepted as such had not the decline of the parliamentary page and the decrease in political coverage been so obvious and their effects so worrying. Similarly, it might have become the accepted form had there not been a parallel concern about the nature of contemporary political coverage in contrast to coverage in an unstated past period: a change from coverage of substance to coverage of gossip, from the story to the story-behind-the-story. Complaints about such changes go far beyond the dates of this present study and were voiced quite commonly in the early to mid-1980s. Once again, we are looking at a gradual process of change which has been taking place over decades rather than years.

To ask searching questions about the media and about parliaments is not to denigrate parliamentary institutions nor to lend support to self-justificatory positions of the media. Nor is it meant to deny the frustrations of legitimately elected parliamentary actors at being ignored and overlooked. Nevertheless others are finding new ways of publicizing themselves and their activities. These questions set out the complex problem of how the world of politics should be covered in the present age, of how the impasse between the political actor and the journalist – with each suspicious of the other – should be overcome. In all these debates, discussions and conversations, it is the public which is often left out, but it is the public which will become the poorer if the sources of political communication make it difficult to 'open windows' onto a full range of information and if political actors become too obsessed with their own world.

Comparisons between newspapers

Although there have been changes in the number of political items coded for each of the five newspapers in the ten-year period analysed here, that change has not been entirely consistent: two of the three British papers

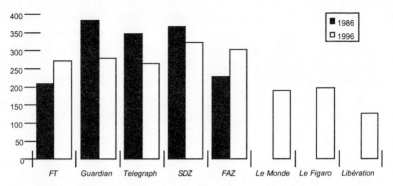

Figure 9.1: Number of political items coded – all newspapers, 1986 and 1996

show a decline in the number of items coded, while the two German papers have moved in opposite directions (Figure 9.1). The French newspapers have fewer coded items in 1996 than any of the other papers and the overall space devoted to these items is generally lower, except for *Le Figaro* which devoted more space to its 190 coded items than did the *SDZ* with its 323 coded items.

In most cases, the total amount of space devoted to all the coded items has increased but that is because of the greater use now being made of larger headlines and more, and larger, photos. If one examines only the space taken up by text, the pattern which emerges simply confirms the

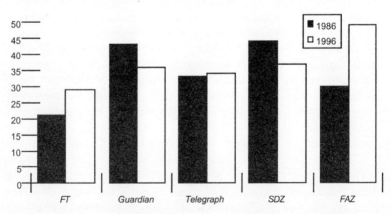

Figure 9.2: Total text space devoted to all coded items ('000 cm. sq.)

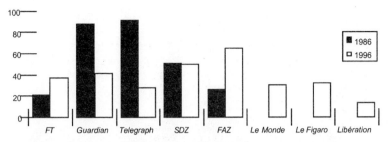

Figure 9.3: Number of items taking place mainly or wholly in parliament, all newspapers

ways in which newspapers have increased, or reduced, their political coverage (Figure 9.2). The *Telegraph* contradicts this statement since it has given more text space to fewer coded political items (see Table 5.1). The data thus confirm that for some newspapers there has been a decline in parliamentary and political reporting, a decline which was exacerbated by the demise of the parliamentary page.

How has the reduction in the number of items coded affected the presence of parliament in the newspapers? Figure 9.3 repeats the pattern seen in the previous two figures. For some newspapers, parliament is less important as a major setting for news stories than in the past – once again, something which has been exacerbated by the demise of the parliamentary page. The other newspapers display a different pattern: the *Financial Times* and the *FAZ* increased their coverage while the *SDZ* remained consistent in its coverage of items taking place in parliament even though it registered an overall decline in the total number of political items coded (from 367 in 1986 to 323 in 1996).

If political coverage for three of the five newspapers has been somewhat downgraded and the range of items given space in newspapers thinned out, would this affect the way newspapers now present themselves to the public? Do their front pages now signal the arrival of less politically 'heavy' newspapers? Table 9.1 compares the number of political items carried on the front pages of the sampled newspapers across the ten years. (The data for the French newspapers in 1986 are missing.)

Table 9.1 confirms, once more, the changing front-page layout of newspapers, but it is important to make one qualification to the data. Although all the newspapers registered a change, the change for the *FAZ* (from 21% to 15%) looks larger in percentage terms than it is in actual numbers of items: the total number of items carried on the front page of the *FAZ*

125

Table 9.1: Percentage of items carried on the front page, all newspapers

	FT	Guardian	Telegraph	SDZ	FAZ	Le Monde	Le Figaro	Libération
1986	13	13	20	13	21	–	–	–
	(13)	(21)	(25)					
1996	11	10	14	10	15	12	5	0
	(10)	(13)	18)					

Note: Percentage of *primary* items carried on front page of the British press in parentheses.

only dropped from 48 to 46, but the overall number of items carried by the paper increased, from 229 to 302. Nevertheless, for the other newspapers, the change leads one to conclude that political items are less likely to make an apperance on front pages today than a decade ago.

How have all these changes affected the coverage of political actors? Certain important qualifications need to be taken into account if comparisons are to be drawn. First, the British data focus on parliamentary and primary political items, that is, items which feature political actors prominently, whereas the other data do not differentiate between primary and secondary political items. Second, the different political systems do not always permit easy comparisons since political roles are differently distributed. For example, the French president and prime minister play a different role from that of the British prime minister and the leader of the opposition. That said, are there any similarities or differences across countries which can be highlighted?

The British data confirm that there are fewer political actors making significant appearances in items coded for both the *Telegraph* and the *Guardian* but not for the *Financial Times* (see Tables 5.3 and 5.4). This same pattern applies to the German newspapers: for the *SDZ*, the decrease is small and from 132 different individuals identified in 1986 to 119 in 1996; for the *FAZ* there was an increase from 89 to 115 (see Tables A8 and A9). The analysis of the French press cannot contribute a great deal in this context given that the data relate to 1996 only, but the available information suggests a lower number of named political actors than in the other papers, with the figures ranging from 71 for *Libération* to 86 for *Le Figaro*. However, the number of coded items is also lower and this may be an important consideration. For all the newspapers, certain key actors (prime minister, president, chancellor) and the government as an entity dominate the lists of members of parliament accessed in the press, so leaving a long list of unknowns.

A short summary of these data suggests that for three of the five newspapers analysed in depth (the *Guardian*, the *Daily Telegraph* and the *SDZ*), political items appear less frequently in 1996 than in 1986 and this has an important impact on the number of political actors making an appearance on those pages. This is not true of the remaining two newspapers, the *Financial Times* and the *FAZ*. Data on the French newspapers do not permit a comparison over the ten years.

Television news content compared

The number of items
For the British television sample, the total number of primary political items coded for the three main television channels declined (from 111 primary items to 94) but the number of secondary items rose from 30 to 43. The change for the German and French channels has been more marked: 67 items down to 36 for ARD, 63 down to 54 for ZDF, 44 down to 25 for TF1, and 42 down to 27 for A2/F2.

In the case of the British sample, the average time devoted to each of these items has increased for all the three main terrestrial channels (Table 6.2). In the case of the German broadcast media, the total time given over to primary political items was reduced but the average length of each item has not – the latter has decreased less dramatically than the former (Table 8.2). As for the French broadcast media, there has been a drop in the average length of each item and in the total time devoted to political items. Whether these changes can be explained by reference to the more intense competition faced by the French and German broadcasters is difficult to say, though that suggestion comes through from some of the work cited above.

The prominence of the coded items
The British primary political items continue to have a prominent position in the news programmes, although there were fewer in the top positions in 1996 than in 1986: the number of primary items featured as either first, second or third item in the news bulletins' running order was 52 stories in 1986 and 42 in 1996. In 1986, eight out of the ten days of Channel 4 news bulletins led with a primary political item. For ITN and BBC1, the respective figure is five days out of ten. In contrast, fewer primary political stories were featured as the first item in 1996, with six out of ten for

127

Channel 4, four out of nine for ITN but six out of ten for BBC1. In German new bulletins, more items featured as first, second and third in 1996 than in 1986. The French data, on the other hand, show a downgrading of political news items: about one-third of all items were featured in the first five positions in 1986, falling to just under 10% in 1996.

Political actors – numbers, locations and time devoted to them
The introduction of television cameras into the British House of Commons helped to change the make-up of political news items. (By contrast, the cameras have been in the other parliaments for much longer – in the case of France from the early 1980s.) This has not meant an increase in the number of actors seen or 'seen and heard' on television. In fact, fewer political actors were seen and 'seen and heard' in 1996 than in 1986, though even then the numbers of actors appearing was small compared to the total number of parliamentary representatives (see Figure 6.3 and Table 6.9, for example).

The pattern for the German media was different: more actors were 'seen and heard' on both channels in 1996 than in 1986 and more were seen on ARD in 1996 than in 1986. Only on ZDF were fewer political actors seen (Table 8.4). In the case of the French broadcast media, more political actors were seen in 1996 than in 1986; more were 'seen and heard' in 1996 in the case of TF1, although the reverse was true for F2 (Table 8.7).

The introduction of cameras into the House of Commons has had an impact on the number of locations in which actors could be seen. Many of the audio-visual extracts from the House came from the two days of the week, Tuesdays and Thursdays, when Prime Minister's Question Time took place. This emphasizes just how newsworthy this set-piece of political theatre has become. For example, on the 11 occasions in 1996 when Tony Blair was seen and heard in the House, five took place on Tuesdays and six on Thursdays. For John Major there is a similar pattern. He was seen and heard on 13 occasions: on Tuesdays (five occasions), Thursdays (six occasions), Monday (once) and Wednesday (once). This degree of concentration was not found in the data for either Germany or France, where parliaments have a different focus, and a focus outside the institution as well as within. In the case of German coverage, there seemed to be a greater focus on the chamber in 1996 and a lessening focus on the other parts of the Bundestag. The French National Assembly is represented in the French data but more important locations appear to be the Elysée Palace and the Matignon.

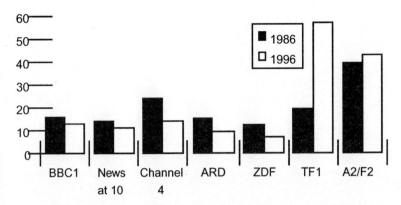

Figure 9.4: Average length of 'seen' appearance, 1986 and 1996 (seconds)

This suggests that broadcast coverage – and press coverage – in each of the countries examined develops out of a particular understanding of what the key political institutions are, who the main actors are and how the various parts of the system interact. Hence the parliamentary show would rank high in the British case; it will also be important in the German case but less so in the French case where other venues (Elysée Palace, Matignon) play an important part in the whole political process.

As regards the amount of time devoted to these political actors, the German and British data point to one pattern, the French to another (Figures 9.4 and 9.5). It is not clear from the available data why the French averages should be out of step with the averages from the two other samples.

In brief, the number of items coded decreased between 1986 and 1996 but they are, nonetheless, still prominent cn national news services. As regards the time allocated to them, there has not been a marked decrease – in fact, the average length of items has often gone up – though the amount of time now taken up by political actors in each of these items has decreased.

Overview

The comparisons made above are only some of the many that would be possible from a study such as this, and they illustrate the patterns which have become apparent from the data. While some British newspapers (for

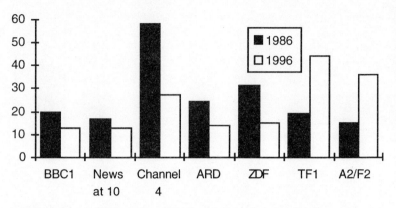

Figure 9.5: Average length of 'seen and heard' appearance, 1986 and 1996 (seconds)

example, the *Guardian* and the *Telegraph*) have moved away from the sorts of political coverage common in the 1980s, the *Financial Times* has broadened its outlook and increased its coverage of politics. The German papers reflect both patterns. Importantly, though, the change which characterized the fall in the number of political items coded for the *SDZ* is more gradual and less obvious than in the case of the British press. The consequences of the change in British press practices with regard to the representation of political actors, and politics and parliament more broadly have already been discussed and can only be reiterated. Once more, the pattern from the German press – the French analysis is more limited here – is different.

As regards television coverage, the main news bulletins on the three main channels in Britain still give politics a prominent position though this is less true for *Sky News* and much less so for regional television. The French sample in 1996 is more like *Sky News* than, say, Channel 4. German broadcasting continues to give prominence to politics, parliament and political actors.

These findings begin to focus on some of the reasons why we should be careful in our assessment of the change. Over time, media change and so do media practices: different designs and layouts, different ways of doing things and different news agendas all affect the final product. This can best be seen in the case of television broadcasting. With television cameras in the chamber, new forms of political communication can take place. The fact that this may not have resulted in a more expansive view of what is going on in the chamber is clearly of concern – except that this concern only raises the question of whether or not the parliamentary institution merits coverage as of right. That said, there is clearly room for a discussion of how much coverage of parliament is made available within the range of items selected by television producers. Is there room for longer extracts? Should journalists be less prominent? These are questions that can be legitimately asked in the light of this, and other, research.

What television viewers would make of all this is something that deserves a study in itself. Have viewers noticed a change? Do they particularly care? Would they resent it – and switch off – if parliamentary institutions were given a higher profile? Would a less confrontational television style on the part of journalists, and MPs, be positively received by the public? Such questions should therefore address both the extent of coverage and the form of political coverage.

The place of political coverage on television news programmes has changed, as the data show, but the change has not been as dramatic as some of the changes recorded for the press. Moreover, it may be that the visibility of political content on television news programmes – near the top of the running order and on most news programmes – gives a greater sense of prominence than would be the case if one scanned the modern newspaper.

In the face of these findings, how does one interpret the sets of concerns which initiated this research? That there has been a change in the extent to which parliament and politics are now covered is undeniable, though one has to qualify that by emphasizing that different media show different trends. What may continue to prompt individuals to complain is the disappearance of a form of journalism which appeared in the past – verbatim reporting – and, if not the disappearance of the form itself – the downgrading of political content; that is, fewer items, less information, and so on. From the point of view of the political actors, much of what they do never appears in the press. What does make an appearance is the newsworthy item. From the point of view of the interested reader, the same is true. Both political actor and interested reader now have less *information* about the institution and its work.

It is here that the full significance of Simon Jenkins's decision becomes clear. His admission that he had decided to do away with the parliamentary page because he could not find anyone apart from Members of Parliament who read it called into question the role of the institution as a source of political comment and information. Jenkins was, in effect, redefining the place of certain forms of coverage in the modern newspaper (and in society) and questioning what had been taken for granted. His supporting statement made this very clear. 'We are not there', he argued, 'to provide a public service for a particular profession or, for that matter, for a particular chamber. ... Newspapers are about providing people with news.'

In this short statement, Jenkins questioned not only the relationship which was assumed to exist between newspapers and parliament, but also the relationship which was assumed to exist between parliament and the public via the press. Parliament and parliamentarians, according to Jenkins, should no longer expect to be covered by the press as a matter of routine. For their part, members of the public should no longer expect their newspapers to carry information about what was going on in parliament or what their elected representatives were doing or saying. Newspapers, as Jenkins put it, were to carry news; dutifully covering the British parliament was a thing of the past, a public service which was now alien to the increasingly competitive and commercial newspaper industry. If broadcasters were to follow suit, as Jenkins has hinted (private correspondence, 1997), then a whole set of assumptions about the role of the media in the political sphere would be in need of a radical revision. Similarly, a whole set of assumptions about the purpose and functions of newspapers would also need to be tackled.

Outsiders surveying the British political scene might find nothing extraordinary in Jenkins's actions. After all, it is unusual to find a newspaper industry where the coverage of the parliamentary institution was organized along the same lines as it had been in Britain until very recently: where space – a page or half-a-page – would consist of nothing more than reproduced accounts of, for example, who had said what in a debate on a particular subject; where members of parliament would find their views *and* words reproduced at some length and not put in context by journalistic or organizational considerations. Admittedly, there may have been a great deal of mythology surrounding the now defunct parliamentary page. The myth had it that what MPs said in the Chamber of the House of Commons (but less often in the Lords!) was dutifully taken down by the ever-present gallery reporter and it would then wind its way into the broadsheet newspaper. The reality was somewhat different, as we have seen: by the early 1900s, coverage of the chamber was anything but *de rigueur*: speeches were often not covered; if covered, they were heavily edited; extracts from speeches were more often than not in the third person, and so on. Despite the evidence which pointed to a gradual decline in parliamentary and political coverage throughout this century, the existence of the parliamentary page was the link with a more glorious, if slightly embroidered, past. Its very existence confirmed the importance of parliament and of MPs.

The action of *The Times* explicitly questioned all this. With the other broadsheets following the pattern it set, there is now no daily record of parliament in the British press. For British parliamentarians, this represented (and represents) a dramatic overturning of their relationship with newspapers: if broadsheet newspapers had once treated parliament in a unique way by giving it guaranteed space in the newspaper, this was no longer the case.

It is impossible to generalize from all this and it would be dangerous to suggest that the trends identified above can also be witnessed elsewhere. The British media are very different from their counterparts in other European countries and so are their relationships with their own parliamentary institutions. As we have seen, it was not until 1989 that the British parliament allowed television cameras into the House of Commons to record debates and committees. By contrast, the West German parliament has been televised since the 1950s. Where the latter institution developed alongside the broadcast media, the former tried to keep the cameras out for as long as possible. This action stemmed from a desire by the British parliament not to have its role and its pre-eminence usurped by the medium of television. In a peculiar way, the existence of the parliamentary page in the broadsheet press supported parliamentary reticence: the public had access to a record of events through the press, television was not needed and, in any case, it would impose its own televisual manners and so somehow distort the parliamentary process. Here, then, was a significant difference between Britain and Germany, among other countries.

Although there have been changes in the two German newspapers selected for this study, these have not been as dramatic, perhaps because the starting points are so very different. In the British case, the period examined is one in which the press had to adapt to the role of television in the House of Commons. In the German case, the period in question has seen no need for such an adaptation because the two media had already coexisted for a long time.

Despite these ups and downs in coverage, it is clear that political actors are by no means absent from newspaper or broadcast news coverage. They still occupy a prominent place in the media, even in Britain's, though perhaps less so than in the recent past. A drop in the number of items is not a sign of total abandonment, perhaps more a sign of a realignment or readjustment in the pattern of coverage. If one adheres to this argument – and it fits in with Simon Jenkins's views – political actors have little to grumble about. This may be true, but only partially so. To understand why it is a partial truth, one needs to remind oneself of what the parliamentary page represented. It was, as has already been argued, a symbol of the pre-eminence of the parliamentary institution and the fact that, being pre-eminent, it deserved to be covered differently. The parliamentary page also confirmed the subservience of the press. Once the press abandoned the parliamentary page, it denied the pre-eminence of parliament. From this, a number of other things followed, the most serious of which was the view that the public need no longer be informed about what parliamentarians did in their daily routines but only when something dramatic happened. The press privileged news over information from the House of Commons; it highlighted certain aspects of the institution – the occasional scandal, the rows, the wrangles – but ignored the routine, the workmanlike, the ordinary. It may be too much to suggest that the ensuing pattern of coverage is in some small way related to public perceptions of parliament and parliamentarians but it is not surprising that parliamentarians object to not having their work reported in a more routine way. They have become, like everyone else, unhappy about how the press reports their lives and their work, although unlike everyone else parliamentarians still have ready access to the media.

The issues touched on above, issues of commercialization and competitive struggles in media sectors, of newspapers popularizing news, of media displacing political content, may have impacted differently in different countries but they have certain things in common. First, they raise questions as to how parliamentary institutions should be covered. Second, how should those who organize our lives explain their actions without interventions by journalists? Third, and equally serious, how can the citizen find out what parliamentarians say and do if there is no routine coverage of the institution?

Such questions will bring forth different answers from different political systems but they will all reflect back on the fundamental issue of democracy, citizenship and the whole process of accountability. Yet these issues have implications beyond national boundaries. For if domestic legislatures appear to be facing problems with media coverage, one needs to spare a thought for the European Parliament: it hardly featured at all in our analysis. What chance that it will find a place in the hearts and minds of European citizens?

Two final points need to be made, related to much that is implicit in the text. The first is the suggestion made by concerned political actors, journalists and academics that things were different in the past. The research reported here – based, admittedly, on a limited sample for the broadcast news media – highlighted some differences between 1986 and 1996. But what was happening in 1976 or 1966? If there has been a change over the last few decades, has it been gradual or dramatic and when did it take place? Similarly, if there has been a change in the style of coverage, in the language and the form of news, when did that take place? Often, journalists are criticized for concentrating on gossip and not the substance of politics. Is it possible to locate this trend? And did it predate 1986?

The second point is more general. If the place of political coverage in the news media is changing, there is an urgent need to consider that change seriously and whether or not it will be detrimental to the legitimately elected political actors, to commentators and to the public at large. Few would suggest a dogmatic approach to this but with new technologies, such as widespread access to the Internet, making different forms of communication possible, perhaps parliamentary actors themselves should consider what the most appropriate channels – or combination of channels – of communication should be.

Bibliography

Blumler, J. (1990) 'Elections, the media and the modern publicity process', in M. Ferguson (ed.), *Public Communication: The New Imperative*. London: Sage, pp. 101–113.

Blumler, J., Franklin, B., Mercer, D. and Tutt, B. (1990) *Monitoring the Public Experiment in Televising the Proceedings of the House of Commons*. Published as the First Report from the Select Committee on the Televising of Proceedings of the House. Session 1989–90, Vol. 1, HC 265-i. London: HMSO.

Chalaby, J. (1996) 'Journalism as an Anglo-American Invention', *European Journal of Communication* 11(3), pp. 303–26. London: Sage.

Charon, J.-M. (1991) *La Presse en France*. Paris: Editions du Seuil.

Cole, J. (1996) 'All Part of the Service', *Guardian*, 4 March 1996, p. 13.

Cook, T. E. (1989) *Making Laws and Making News Media Strategies in the US House of Representatives*. Washington, DC: Brookings Institution.

CSA (Conseil Supérieur de l'Audiovisuel), Paris.

Engel, M. (1996) *Tickle the Public: One Hundred Years of the Popular Press*. London: Cassell.

Franklin, B. (1995a) 'Parliament on the spike?' Paper given at the Political Studies Association, University of York, April 1995.

Franklin, B. (1995b) 'Newspaper Reporting of Parliament'. Final Report, unpublished paper.

Franklin, B. (ed.) (1992) *Televising Democracies*. London: Routledge.

Frears, J. (1990) 'The French Parliament: Loyal Workhorse, Poor Watchdog', *West European Politics* 13(3), pp. 32–51. London: Frank Cass.

Fundesco/Association of European Journalists (1997) *The European Union in the Media 1996*. Madrid: Fundesco.

Gould, B. (1984) 'Televise Parliament to Halt the Decline', *Parliamentary Affairs* 37(3), pp. 243–49. Oxford: OUP.

136

Hennis, W. (1971) 'Reform of the Bundestag: the case for general debate', in Loewenberg (ed.), *Modern Parliaments*.

Hess, S. (1994) 'The decline and fall of Congressional news', in Mann and Orenstein, *Congress, the Press and the Public*.

Hess, S. (1993) 'Public opinion and the decline of legislative news in the United States'. Unpublished paper, Madrid, August 1993.

Hess, S. (1986) *The Ultimate Insiders: US Senators in the National Media*. Washington, DC: Brookings Institution.

Hill, P. (1993) 'Parliamentary Broadcasting – from TWIW to YIP', *British Journalism Review* 4(4), pp. 39–44. London: BJR Publishing.

Humphreys, P. (1996) *Mass Media and Media Policy in Western Europe*. Manchester: Manchester University Press.

Jenkins, S. (1995) in First Report of the Committee on Standards in Public Life (Chair: Lord Nolan). Vol. 2; Transcripts of Oral Evidence, Cm 2850-II, London, HMSO, p. 7

Jones, N. (1996) *Soundbites and Spin Doctors*. London: Indigo.

Kuhn, Raymond (1994) *The Media in France*. London: Routledge.

Kynaston, D. (1988) *The Financial Times. A Centenary History*. London: Viking.

Lee, A. (1976) *The Origins of the Popular Press 1855–1914*. London: Croom Helm.

Loewenberg, G. (1971) *Modern Parliaments: Change or Decline?*. New York: Aldine.

Mann, T. and Orenstein, N. (eds) (1994) *Congress, the Press, and the Public*. Washington, DC: AEI/ Brookings Institution.

Mayntz, G. (1993) 'Dokumentation und Kurzanalysen. Die Fernsehberichterstattung über den Deutschen Bundestag. Eine Bilanz', *Zeitschrift für Parlamentsfragen*. 3/93. (Documentation and Brief Analysis (Summary). Summary of Television Reportage of the German Lower House.)

McDonald, S. (1994) *Guardian,* 14 December.

McQuail, D. (1977) *Analysis of Newspaper Content*. Cmnd 6810-4, London: HMSO.

Negrine, R. (1996) *The Communication of Politics*. London: Sage.

Negrine, R. (1994) *Politics and the Mass Media in Britain* (2nd edn), London: Routledge.

Negrine, R. (1992) 'Parliamentary Select Committees and the Media: a case study of the British Aerospace takeover of the Rover Group', *Parliamentary Affairs*, 45(3), pp. 399–408. Oxford: OUP.

Norton, P. (1993) *Does Parliament Matter?*. London: Harvester Wheatsheaf.

Oberreuter, H. (1990) 'The Bundestag and Media in the Federal Republic of Germany', in Thaysen et al., *The US Congress and the German Bundestag*.

Padioleau, J.-G. (1985) *Le Monde et le Washington Post*. Paris: Presses Universitaires de France.

Paterson, W. and Southern, D. (1991) *Governing Germany*. Oxford: Blackwell.

Pfetsch, B. (1996) 'Convergence through privatization? Changing media environments and televised politics in Germany', *European Journal of*

Communication 11(4), pp. 427–52.

Ryle, M. (1991) 'Televising the Commons', *Parliamentary Affairs*, pp. 185–207.

Schatz, H. (1992) 'Televising the Bundestag', in Franklin, B., *Televising Democracies*. London: Routledge, pp. 234–53.

Seymour-Ure, C. (1977) 'Parliament and Government', in Boyd-Barrett, O., Seymour-Ure, C. and Tunstall, J., *Studies on the Press*. London: HMSO, pp. 83–158.

Seymour-Ure, C. (1979) 'Parliament and Mass Communication in the Twentieth Century', in Walkland, S. (ed.), *The House of Commons in the Twentieth Century*. Oxford: Clarendon Press. pp. 527–95.Spender, J. (1927) *Life, Journalism and Politics,* Vol. 1. London: Cassell.

Steed, W. (1938) *The Press*. London: Penguin special.

Stevens, A. (1992) *The Government and Politics of France*. London: Macmillan.

Straw, J. (1993) *The Decline in Press Reporting of Parliament*. October 1993. London.

Taras, D. (1996) 'The new and old worlds: media coverage and legislative politics in Canada'. Unpublished paper.

Thaysen, U., Davidson, R. and Livingston, R. (1990) *The US Congress and the German Bundestag*. Boulder, CO: Westview Press.

Thibau, J. (1996) *Le Monde 1944–1996: Histoire d'un Journal, Un Journal dans l'Histoire*. Paris: Plon.

Tidmarch, C. (1990) 'Legislators and Media Producers: Congress and Communication in the US', in Thaysen et al., *The US Congress and the German Bundestag*.

Wilson, C. (1970) *Parliaments, Peoples and the Media*. London: Cassell.

Appendix I

The media sample

Content analysis of newspapers

For both 1986 and 1996, 15 issues of newspapers were selected on a rolling week basis. In week 1, a Monday issue was chosen, in week 2, a Tuesday issue, week 3, a Wednesday issue, and so on. The issues selected are identified in the table below.

The British team also looked at ten issues taken from a two-week period in 1989. This period was identical to the period of the television analysis for 1989. A little of these data features in this monograph.

One reason for a more limited analysis of 1989, apart from time and resource constraints, was that preliminary work suggested that 1989 was not significantly different from the 1986 period to warrant more detailed analysis. In other words, the real contrast was between 1986 and 1996.

1996		*1986*	
Tuesday	9 January	Tuesday	7 January
Wednesday	17 January	Wednesday	15 January
Thursday	25 January	Thursday	23 January
Friday	2 February	Friday	31 January
Monday	5 February	Monday	3 February
Tuesday	13 February	Tuesday	11 February
Wednesday	21 February	Wednesday	19 February
Thursday	29 February	Thursday	27 February
Friday	8 March	Friday	7 March
Monday	11 March	Monday	10 March
Tuesday	19 March	Tuesday	18 March

Appendix I

1996		*1986*	
Wednesday	27 March	Wednesday	26 March
Thursday	4 April	Thursday	3 April
Friday	12 April	Friday	11 April
Monday	15 April	Monday	14 April

Newspapers analysed:
Britain: *Guardian, Financial Times, Daily Telegraph*
Germany: *Frankfurter Allegmeine Zeitung, Süddeutsche Zeitung*
France: *Le Figaro, Le Monde, Libération* (only for 1996)

Broadcast output analysed

Britain
1986: 7–11 July, 27–31 October
1996: 19–23 February, 18–22 March

The British broadcast media analysed included:
Radio 4, *The World at One*; *Central News*; BBC, *Midlands Today*; BBC1, *Nine O'Clock News*; ITN, *News at Ten*; Channel 4, *Channel Four News.*

Sky News was also analysed in the two week period in 1996, and a period in 1989 was also analysed.

Germany
1986: 23–27 June, 22–26 September
1996: 6–10 May, 10–14 June (for ARD only), 24–28 June (ZDF only)

The German broadcast media analysed included:
Arbeitsgemeinschaft der Rundfunkanstalten Deutschlands (ARD) and Zweites Deutsches Fernsehen (ZDF).

France
1986: 7–11 July, 27–31 October
1996: 22–26 January, 19–23 February

The French broadcast media analysed included:
Antenne 2/France 2 (A2/F2) and Télévision Française 1 (TF1).

140

Appendix 2

Supplementary tables

Table A1a: Photos in primary items

Paper		No. of items with photos	% of items with photos	Total cm. sq. given to photos
Telegraph 86	n = 206	12	6	1,170
Telegraph 96	n = 163	36	22	5,939
Guardian 86	n = 208	43	21	3,722
Guardian 96	n = 171	42	25	9,491
FT 86	n = 127	12	9	426
FT 96	n = 147	24	16	3,426

Table A1b: Photos in secondary items

Telegraph 86	n = 73	5	7	443
Telegraph 96	n = 92	29	32	5,309
Guardian 86	n = 102	10	10	689
Guardian 96	n = 101	27	27	6,868
FT 86	n = 50	5	10	202
FT 96	n = 92	17	18	2141

Table A1c: Average (mean) size of headline in primary items (sq. cm.)

	Average size of headline in 1986	Average size of headline in 1996
Guardian	40	64
Financial Times	37	50
Telegraph	28	53

Table A2a: General focus or description of items, *Financial Times*

	1986 Primary and parliamentary		1996 Primary and parliamentary		1986 Secondary		1996 Secondary	
	n = 127	%	n = 147	%	n = 50	%	n = 92	%
Primarily political, social and economic items	93	73	113	77	20	40	27	29
Items about N. Ireland	6	5	9	6	1	2	6	7
News about EU/Commission/ directives	1	1	1	1	3	6	12	13
News about countries and EU relations (not British)	–	–	–	–	3	6	–	–
Individual countries and Britain	19	15	1	1	10	20	–	–
EU as it relates to Britain	3	2	7	5	1	2	3	3
Other home news abroad	4	3	5	3	1	2	4	4
Other	1	1	11	7	11	22	40	43

Table A2b: General focus or description of items, *Guardian*

	1986 Primary and parliamentary		1996 Primary and parliamentary		1986 secondary		1996 secondary	
	n = 273	%	n = 171	%	n = 102	%	n = 101	%
Primarily political, social and economic items	203	74	125	73	71	70	31	31
Items about N. Ireland	12	4	15	9	3	3	8	8
News about EU/Commission/ directives	2	1	1	1	2	2	7	7
News about countries and EU relations (not British)	–	–	–	–	1	1		
Individual countries and Britain	16	6	1	1	9	9	1	1
EU as it relates to Britain	5	2	12	7	2	2	3	3
Other home news abroad	4	1	6	4	2	2	2	2
Other	3	1	11	6	13	13	48	48

Table A2c: General focus or description of items, *Daily Telegraph*

	1986 Primary and parliamentary items		1996 Primary and parliamentary items		1986 Secondary		1996 Secondary	
	n = 26 2%		n = 16 3%		n = 73 %		n = 92 %	
Primarily political, social and economic items	217	83	115	71	57	78	18	20
Items about N. Ireland	13	5	18	11	4	5	9	10
News about EU/Commission directives	6	2	1	1	1	1	17	18
news about countries and EU relations (not British)	–	–	–	–	–	–	–	–
individual countries and Britain	17	6	1	1	4	5		
EU as it relates to Britain	8	3	9	5	5	7	3	3
Other home news abroad	3	1	13	8	–	–	5	5
Other	1	–	6	4	2	3	40	43

Table A3a: Primary political and parliamentary items coded by the first main subject of item, as percentage of total primary items*

Financial Times

	Primary 1986 n = 127	%	Primary 1996 n = 147	%
General political	8	6	27	18
Ireland	5	4	11	8
Economic policy	37	29	24	16
Health	–	–	4	3
Social security/services	2	2	4	3
Education	2	2	9	6
Leisure: arts, media, etc.	3	2	8	5
Law and order/crime	4	3	4	3
European issues	4	3	6	4
Britain's relations with Europe	5	4	4	3
Foreign news	5	4	2	1
Local government	6	5	3	2
Westland affair	10	8	–	–
BSE	–	–	7	5
Defence	8	6	1	1
Financial news	9	7	6	4
Transport	1	1	5	3
Other	10	8	6	4
Total items	119	94% of total items	131	89% of total items

*Data relate to main subjects. Many items in other subject categories occurred very infrequently as individual items.

Table A3b: Primary political and parliamentary items coded by the first main subject of item, as percentage of total primary items*

Guardian

	Primary 1986 n = 208	%	Parliamentary 1986 n = 65	%	Primary 1996 n = 171	%
General political	18	9	5	8	26	15
Ireland	12	6	1	2	15	9
Economic policy	45	22	10	15	19	11
Health	5	2	1	2	8	5
Social security/services	5	2	2	3	6	4
Education	10	5	5	8	14	8
Leisure: arts, media, etc.	6	3	4	6	8	5
Law and order/crime	18	9	3	5	14	8
European issues	1	1	1	2	–	–
Britain's relations with Europe	5	2	1	2	14	8
Foreign news	6	3	2	3	3	2
Local government	13	6	3	5	–	–
Westland affair	17	8	5	8	–	–
BSE	–	–	–	–	8	5
Defence	9	4	3	5	1	1
Financial news	4	2	–	–	–	–
Transport	4	2	–	–	3	2
Other	7	3	7	3	6	4
Total items	185	89% of total items	53	82% of total items	145	85% of total items

145

Table A3c: Primary political and parliamentary items coded by the first main subject of item, as percentage of total primary items*

Daily Telegraph

	Primary 1986 n = 206	%	Parliamentary 1986 n = 59	%	Primary 1986 n = 163	%
General political	21	10	3	5	30	18
Ireland	13	6	3	5	22	13
Economic policy	35	17	9	15	11	7
Health	7	3	2	3	4	2
Social security/services	3	1	3	5	6	4
Education	10	5	6	10	6	4
Leisure: arts, media, etc.	2	1	–	–	10	6
Law and order/crime	14	7	3	5	11	7
European issues	4	2	–	–	5	3
Britain's relations with Europe	9	4	–	–	3	2
Foreign news	8	4	1	2	1	1
Local government	11	5	6	10	1	1
Westland affair	17	8	5	8	–	–
BSE	–	–	–	–	7	4
Defence	3	1	3	5	6	4
Financial news	5	2	3	5	4	2
Transport	10	5	2	3	1	1
Other	13	6	3	5	7	4
Total items	185	90%	52	88%	135	83%
	of total items		of total items		of total items	

Table A4: Number and percentage of items with their focus in parliament or government

	FT 86	FT 96	DT 86	DT 96	Gdn 86	Gdn 96
Parliamentary focus, inc. PMQT, debates, statements, etc.	18 14%	25 17%	25 12% (45)	30 18%	26 13% (41)	25 15%
Parliamentary committees	7 6%	14 10%	14 7% (4)	13 8%	8 4% (3)	8 5%
House of Lords	3 2%	5 3%	4 2% (4)	2 1%	3 2% (14)	2 1%
Total parliamentary	**28** **22%**	**44** **30%**	**43** **21%** **(53)**	**45** **27%**	**37** **18%** **(58)**	**35** **20%**
Government or departmental announcements, reports, etc.	34 27%	20 14%	42 20% (1)	16 9%	25 12%	16 10%
Downing St location	2 2%	5 3%	5 2%	4 2%	2 1%	5 3%
Outside parliament	– 	20 14%	– 	21 12%	– 	20 12%
Can't determine location	12 9%	37 25%	26 13%	31 18%	50 24%	37 23%
Total primary items	**127**	**147**	**206** **(59)**	**163**	**208** **(65)**	**171**

Note: Number of parliamentary page items included in parentheses.

Table A5: Items and how much of the item is located in parliament, 1996

1996	Total items	Percentage under 50% in parliament	Percentage 51–100% in parliament	Can't determine location (%)
FT primary items	147	7	25	30
Guardian primary items	171	10	22	18
Telegraph primary items	163	10	17	23

Table A6a: Items and how much of item consists of quotes, 1986

1986	Total items	Percentage under 50%	Percentage 51–100%	Percentage with no quotes
FT Primary items	127	57	2	41
Guardian primary items	208	60	6	34
Guardian parliamentary page	65	68	8	24
Telegraph primary items	206	66	5	29
Telegraph parliamentary page	59	71	14	15

Table A6b: Items and how much of item consists of quotes, 1996

1996	Total items	Percentage under 50%	Percentage 51–100%	Percentage with no quotes
FT Primary items	147	81	2	17
Guardian primary items	171	81	3	16
Telegraph primary items	163	77	6	18

Table A7: Number of mentions of named political actors, primary political items only, 1986

Financial Times (Total items, n = 127)

Actor/Position	1	2	3	4	5	6	7
Government	39	23	14	10	3	2	1
Cons. Party	22	18	22	19	18	15	8
Labour Party	2	2	5	2	2	3	3
Lib. Dems.	–	1	4	4	2	–	–

Guardian (Total items, n = 208)

Actor/Position	1	2	3	4	5	6	7
Government	45	33	14	12	6	4	5
Cons. Party	38	36	40	32	32	27	25
Labour Party	9	7	8	10	6	8	10
Lib. Dems.	4	3	5	4	5	4	1

Telegraph (Total items, n = 206)

Actor/Position	1	2	3	4	5	6	7
Government	38	33	17	6	3	8	1
Cons. Party	50	47	34	27	35	11	12
Labour Party	7	9	7	14	3	4	6
Lib. Dems.	1	1	4	2	2	2	1

Table A8: Major Conservative political actors referred to, 1986

Financial Times

Actor/Position	1	2	3	4	5	6	7
Thatcher (Prime Minister)	7	5	2	4	3	4	1
Lawson (Chancellor)	3	3	3	2	–	–	–
Howe (Foreign Secretary)	2	–	1	1	1	–	–
Hurd (Home Secretary)	1	–	2	–	2	–	–
Channon (Trade and Industry)	–	–	3	–	1	1	–
Brittan (Trade and Industry)	–	–	4	1	2	–	–
Heseltine	1	1	1	2	–	–	3
Total mentions	14	9	16	10	9	5	4
Others	6	9	6	9	9	10	4

Guardian, 1986

Actor/Position	1	2	3	4	5	6	7
Thatcher (Prime Minister)	14	10	8	6	5	9	2
Lawson (Chancellor)	3	–	4	1	–	2	1
Howe (Foreign Secretary)	3	–	1	2	2	1	1
Hurd (Home Secretary)	1	2	2	3	–	–	1
Channon (Trade and Industry)	1	1	–	–	1	2	1
Brittan (Trade and Industry)	3	4	2	3	2	–	3
Heseltine	1	4	2	2	1	2	–
Total mentions	26	21	19	17	11	16	9
Others	12	15	13	15	21	11	16

Telegraph

Actor/Position	1	2	3	4	5	6	7
Thatcher (Prime Minister)	14	12	6	4	5	2	1
Lawson (Chancellor)	2	3	–	–	2	–	2
Howe (Foreign Secretary)	3	2	2	1	2	–	–
Hurd (Home Secretary)	3	1	2	1	2	–	–
Channon (Trade and Industry)	–	4	1	1	2	–	–
Brittan (Trade and Industry)	3	–	4	–	5	–	–
Heseltine	3	2	3	3	3	1	–
Joseph (Education)	4	1	–	–	–	2	1
Total	32	25	18	10	21	5	4
Others	21	20	15	15	13	6	7

Table A9: Conservative political actors appearing in positions 1 to 7 of primary political items, 1996

Financial Times, n = 147

Actor/Position	1	2	3	4	5	6	7
'The government'	42	10	14	8	10	4	9
Major (PM)	9	6	3	3	3	2	2
Howard (Home Secretary)	–	2	2	2	–	1	–
Clarke (Chancellor)	3	3	2	1	1	–	1
Heseltine (Deputy PM)	5	3	2	–	–	1	1
Rifkind	3	2	–	–	1	–	1
Total mentions of politicians (exc. general categories and 'the government')	38	24	20	18	10	12	12

Guardian, n = 171

Actor/Position	1	2	3	4	5	6	7
'The government'	29	19	11	9	8	8	4
Major (PM)	12	8	6	5	5	2	3
Howard (Home Secretary)	7	2	–	–	1	–	–
Clarke (Chancellor)	–	–	2	–	–	–	1
Heseltine (Deputy PM)	2	2	2	1	1	–	–
Rifkind	1	1	–	1	–	1	2
Total mentions of politicians (exc. general categories and 'the government')	35	33	28	21	21	19	18

Telegraph, n = 162

Actor/Position	1	2	3	4	5	6	7
'The government'	25	17	15	7	11	3	7
Major (PM)	11	6	7	2	2	3	3
Howard (Home Secretary)	7	5	–	–	1	–	–
Clarke (Chancellor)	2	–	–	1	–	–	1
Heseltine (Deputy PM)	3	2	–	1	1	2	1
Rifkind	–	1	1	–	2	–	–
Total mentions of politicians (exc. general categories and 'the government')	39	15	18	16	16	13	16

Table A10: Coverage of Labour Party actors, 1986

Financial Times

Actor/Position	1	2	3	4	5	6	7
Kinnock (Opp. leader)	–	–	2	–	1	1	1
Hattersley (Deputy)	1	–	1	–	–	–	–
Smith	1	–	–	–	–	1	–
Total	2	–	3	–	1	2	1
Others	–	2	2	2	1	1	2

Guardian

Actor/Position	1	2	3	4	5	6	7
Kinnock (Opp. leader)	2	–	1	2	2	–	3
Hattersley (Deputy)	–	1	1	1	1	1	–
Smith	–	1	–	–	–	–	–
Straw	–	1	–	2	–	1	–
Total	2	3	2	5	3	2	3
Others	7	4	6	5	3	5	7

Telegraph

Actor/Position	1	2	3	4	5	6	7
Kinnock (Opp. leader)	2	2	2	6	–	1	–
Hattersley (Deputy)	3	1	–	1	–	–	1
Smith	–	–	1	–	–	–	–
Straw	–	–	–	–	1	–	–
Total	5	3	3	7	1	1	1
Others	2	6	4	7	2	3	5

Table A11: Coverage of Labour Party actors, 1996 (relative to PM)

Financial Times

Actor/Position	1	2	3	4	5	6	7
Blair	5	1	1	2	2	–	3
Prescott	–	1	–	1	–	1	–
Harman	–	–	1	1	–	1	–
Total mentions (exc. general references)	6	6	5	11	8	6	6
Major (PM)	9	6	3	4	3	2	2

Guardian

Actor/Position	1	2	3	4	5	6	7
Blair	6	4	5	5	2	2	4
Prescott	–	1	–	–	–	3	1
Harman	4	–	2	4	1	–	2
Total mentions (exc. general references)	16	11	16	17	10	15	16
Major (PM)	12	8	3	2	5	2	3

Telegraph 1996

Actor/Position	1	2	3	4	5	6	7
Blair	6	5	1	1	2	–	2
Prescott	–	–	–	–	–	–	–
Harman	1	–	1	–	1	–	1
Total mentions (exc. general references)	13	7	6	3	7	5	4
Major (PM)	11	6	3	2	3	2	3

Table A12: Political actors seen and heard in primary news items, by political party (excluding House of Lords)

		1986			1996	
	BBC1*	ITN	Channel 4	BBC1	ITN*	Channel 4
Conservative	1,097**	932	2,595***	516	545	1,593
Party actors	77%	68%	56%	51%	68%	67%
Labour Party	184	331	1,517	180	158	524
actors	13%	24%	33%	18%	20%	22%
Liberal	56	59	273	86	19	71
Alliance/	4%	4%	6%	9%	2%	3%
Lib. Dems.						
Others	92	53	206	225	74	214
	6%	4%	5%	22%	9%	9%

*   9 bulletins only.

**   123 seconds are repeated as two actors appear together.

***   173 seconds are repeated as two actors appear together.

Table A13: Total number of locations featuring individual actors, 1986

Actor	Total number of appearances in all locations	Percentage of appearances at each location
Prime Minister	30 (i.e. PM made appearances in 27 items, and these showed her in 30 locations)	20% in and around Downing St; 10% audio from chamber; 13% as photo in TV studio; 53% other location; 3% EU location.
Home Secretary	3	33% in and around Downing St; 67% as photo in TV studio.
Foreign Secretary	36	8% in and around Downing St; 6% audio from chamber; 28% as photo/ interviewed in studio; 31% other location; 28% EU location.
Northern Ireland Secretary	3	33% as photo in TV studio; 67% other location.
Leader of Opposition	15	7% in environs of Commons; 20% audio from chamber; 47% as photo in TV studio; 27% other location.
David Owen (SDP leader)	3	67% as photo/interviewed in studio; 33% other location.
David Steel (Liberal leader)	6	33% audio from chamber; 50% as photo in studio; 17% other location.

Table A14: Total number of locations featuring individual actors, 1996

Actor	Total number of appearances in all locations	Percentage of appearances at each location
Prime Minister	37	22% in and around Downing St; 51% seen and heard in chamber; 3% as photo in TV studio; 22 % other location; 3% EU location.
Home Secretary	14	21% in and around Downing St; 36% as photo/interviewed in studio; 29% other location; 14% EU location.
Foreign Secretary	3	33% in and around Downing St; 67% seen and heard in Committee in Westminster.
Northern Ireland Secretary	5	40% in and around Downing St; 60% seen and heard in chamber.
Leader of Opposition	20	75% seen and heard in chamber; 5% as photo in TV studio; 20% other location.
Paddy Ashdown (Lib. Dem. leader)	6	100% seen and heard in chamber.

Table A15: Politicians seen and seen/heard on Sky News, 1996 sample (seconds)

	Seen in chamber	Seen/heard in chamber	Seen elsewhere	Seen/heard elsewhere	Other
John Major	29	69	54	21	14 (voice-over)
Tony Blair	11	20	12	–	–
Paddy Ashdown	12	8	–	–	–
Others (named)	27	83	99	147	
Others (unnamed)	–	24	8*		
TOTAL	79	204	173	168	14
General visuals from chamber	40				

*Immediately outside the House of Commons.

Table A16: Some key political actors seen, and 'seen and heard', in 1989 (seconds)

Political actor	Seen	Seen and heard
Margaret Thatcher	117	59
Neil Kinnock		78
Geoffrey Howe	41	9
Edward Heath	11	116
Paddy Ashdown	7	7
Clarke	25	89
Total all political actors	436	789

Table A17: Main subjects of coded items, German newspapers (%)

	SDZ 1986	SDZ 1996	FAZ 1986	FAZ 1996
General political	5	5	9	8
Political development ('old' states)	26	17	22	9
Political development ('new' states)	–	6	–	10
Economic policy, industry/employment	5	19	7	16
Civil liberties	5	3	8	3
European issues (domestic)	6	7	4	10
European issues (abroad)	10	7	12	8
Scandals	2	1	1	2
Law and order	3	4	3	3
Total percentage	62	69	66	69

Table A18: First location of coded items, German newspapers

	SDZ 1986 n = 367	SDZ 1996 n = 323	FAZ 1986 n = 229	FAZ 1996 n = 302
In parliament	14%	12%	16%	18%
(Federal Chancellor, etc.)	(53 items)	(38 items)	(37 items)	(53 items)
Parliamentary committees	1%	–	2%	–
Outside parliament	31%	28%	34%	22%
(Federal Chancellor, etc.)	(113 items)	(92 items)	(77 items)	(67 items)
Federal states (other political actors)	9%	7%	9%	8%
Overseas (Chancellor, Ministers)	3%	3%	4%	2%
Departments	5%	10%	4%	9%
EU Commission	5%	8%	3%	12%
	(17 items)	(25 items)	(8 items)	(36 items)
Länder parliaments	7%	6%	4%	6%
Others	8%	6%	4%	8%
Not applicable	14%	16%	15%	11%
Total	97%	97%	96%	96%

Table A19: References to main political actors: German groupings, 1986 and 1996 (%)

Süddeutsche Zeitung

	Mention in 1st position n = 367	Mention in 2nd position n = 367	Mention in 1st position n = 323	Mention in 2nd position n = 323
Chancellor	2	1	1	1
Ministers	21	8	18	8
Government party	5	3	5	5
Opposition party	8	3	6	4
Länder states-ministers and presidents	7	1	5	3
Ministers etc. in *Länder*	9	4	10	4
Länder parliaments	5	3	3	2

Frankfurter Allgemeine Zeitung

	Mention in 1st position n = 229	Mention in 2nd position n = 229	Mention in 1st position n = 302	Mention in 2nd position n = 302
Chancellor	4	2	1	–
Ministers	23	8	21	9
Government party	9	4	5	4
Opposition party	5	5	5	3
Länder states-ministers and presidents	76	1	6	2
Ministers etc. in *Länder*	910	4	7	6
Länder parliaments	52	3	4	4

Table A20: Number of times key individual political actors identified in first two positions in German newspapers, all items, 1986

	SDZ 1986, n = 367 first placing	SDZ 1986, n = 367 second placing	FAZ 1986, n = 229 first placing	FAZ 1986, n = 229 second placing
Strauss*	9 mentions	2	I	I
Bangemann*	8	3	4	I
Sprecher*	8	6	I	–
Kohl*	6	3	8	5
Dollinger*	5	I	I	–
Hiersmann	5	–	I	–
Blum*	5	3	3	2
Rau*	5	–	2	–
Schneider*	5	–	2	I
Sunsmuth*	5	–	2	I
Vogel, V.	5	I	3	3
Genscher,*	4	2	4	I
Zimmerman*	4	I	5	–
Kiechle*	I	–	4	I
Other actors	5 mentioned three times	– mentioned three times	2 mentioned three times	I mentioned three times
Other actors	17 mentioned twice each	6 mentioned twice each	11 mentioned twice	3 mentioned twice
Governmental and group actors (not named)	37 mentions	19 mentions	32 mentions	18 mentions
Total individual political actors identified	132	73	89	48
Total individual political actors mentioned	227 times	91	133	59
Total mentions	264	110	165	77

*Ministers in various capacities.

Table A21: Number of times key individual political actors identified in first two positions in German newspapers, all items, 1996

	SDZ 1996, n = 323	SDZ 1996, n = 323	FAZ 1996, n = 302	FAZ 1996, n = 302
Kinkel	5	–	6	4
Kohl	4	3	4	I
Lafontaine	4	I	2	4
Merkel	4	I	3	–
Beckstein	4	I	I	–
Ruttgers	5	–	2	–
Scharping	5	I	2	2
Schmidt-Jortzig	5	I	2	–
Sprecher	4	3	3	I
Stoiber	4	I	2	–
Waigel	3	3	3	3
Rexrodt	3	4	9	I
Seehofer	3	I	2	–
Simonis	3	4	3	–
Teufel	–	–	4	–
Other actors	3 mentioned three times	– mentioned three times	– mentioned three times	2 mentioned three times
Other actors	18 mentioned twice each	5 mentioned twice each	4 mentioned twice	5 mentioned twice
Governmental and group actors (not named)	33 mentions	17 mentions	48 mentions	34 mentions
Total individual political actors identified	119	81	115	77
Total individual political actors mentioned	182	96	156	92
Total mentions	215	113	204	126

Appendix 2

Table A22: Total number of political actors quoted in German newspapers, all items, first position only

1986 actors	SDZ 1986, n = 367	FAZ 1986, n = 229	1996 actors	SDZ 1996, n = 323	FAZ 1996, n = 302
Strauss	9	–	Kinkel	5	6
Bangemann	8	4	Kohl	4	4
Sprecher	9	1	Lafontaine	3	–
Kohl	6	8	Merkel	3	3
Dollinger	4	1	Ruttgers	4	1
Hiersmann	5	1	Scharping	4	2
Blum	5	3	Schmidt-Jortzig	4	2
Schneider	5	2	Sprecher	7	6
Rau	5	2	Stoiber	4	2
Sunsmuth	5	2	Beckstein	4	1
Vogel, V.	5	3	Rexrodt	1	5
Genscher	2	4	Waigel	3	2
Zimmerman	4	5	Simonis	3	3
Stoltenberg	3	4	Teufel	2	4
Kiechle	1	3	–	–	–
Other actors quoted 3 times	4	1		3	–
Other actors quoted 2 times	18	10		19	5
Govt. and group actors (not named)	29	20		30	17
Other individual political actors quoted once	127	80		132	124
Total number of actors quoted	**240**	**116**		**183**	**163**

All those listed were either federal ministers or held other positions of political responsibility.

162

Table A23: All items by main subject, French newspapers, 1996 (%)

	Le Figaro, n = 196	Le Monde, n = 190	Libération, n = 128
Politics, general	22	11	24
	44 items	21 items	31 items
22 11	24		
Politics and economic policy	8	9	9
Health	4	3	2
Transport	2	1	1
Social security	7	2	6
Law and order	4	4	2
European issues (domestic)	4	5	8
European issues (overseas)	11	16	8
Sleaze	1	2	6
Education	3	5	6
Defence	6	5	5
Total	72	63	77

Table A24: Number of references to categories of actors in French newspapers, first three positions only, all items

Le Figaro, n = 196

Position	I	%	2	%	3	%
Chirac, J. (Pres.)	4	2	5	3	3	2
Juppé, A. (PM)	23	12	9	5	6	3
PR (Parti Républicain)	12	6	4	2	4	2
Government and Ministers	55	28	22	11	10	5
RPR (Rassemblement pour la République)	7	4	12	6	6	3
'The left'	6	3	7	4	8	4
UDF (Federation of parties)	7	4	8	4	11	6
EC/EU bodies	18	9	13	7	11	6
European parliament	2	1	3	2	3	2
Total – rows I to 7		**59**		**35**		**25**

Le Monde, n = 190

	I	%	2	%	3	%
Chirac	8	4	8	4	6	3
Juppé	18	10	16	8	7	4
PR	3	2	5	3	4	2
Government and Ministers	47	25	24	13	25	13
RPR	8	4	6	3	–	
'The left'	9	5	6	3	7	4
UDF	4	2	3	2	3	2
EC/EU bodies	16	8	15	8	10	5
EP –			2	1	2	1
Total – rows I to 7		**52**		**36**		**28**

Libération, n = 128

	I	%	2	%	3	%
Chirac	8	6	4	3	5	4
Juppé	19	15	8	6	5	4
PR	8	6	5	4	3	2
Government and Ministers	26	20	23	18	15	12
RPR	6	5	3	2	5	4
'The left'	12	9	12	9	8	6
UDF	3	2	5	4	2	2
EC/EU bodies	4	3	4	3	4	3
EP	2		–		1	